AF430236

This Handwriting
workbook belongs to :

Step 1:

Learning Letters

Trace the letters and practice writing them in the remaining space.

For more fun, each letter includes a cute image that you can color.

Are you ready?

Let's Go!!

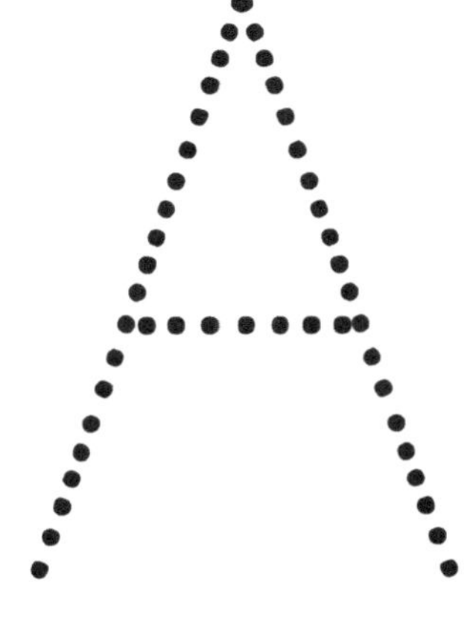

is for Apple

Trace the cursive letters, then write your own

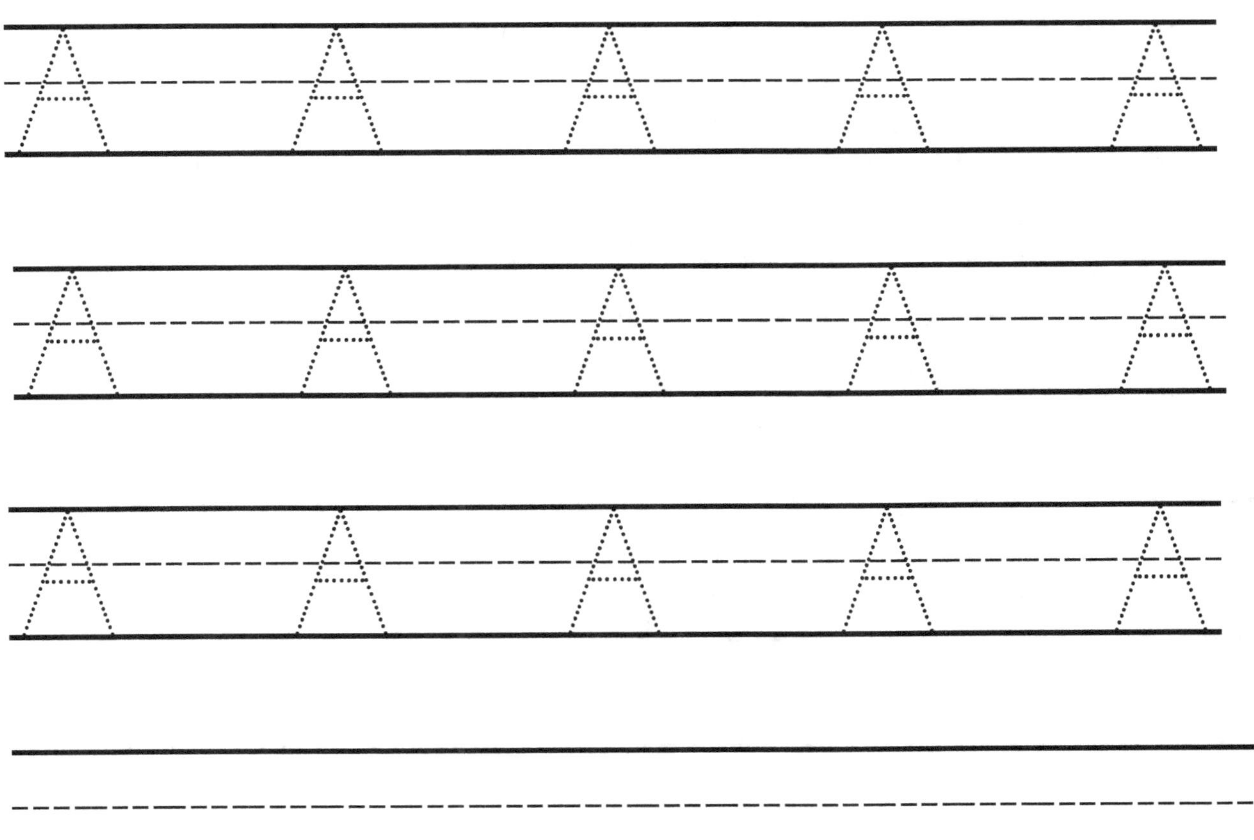

is for apple

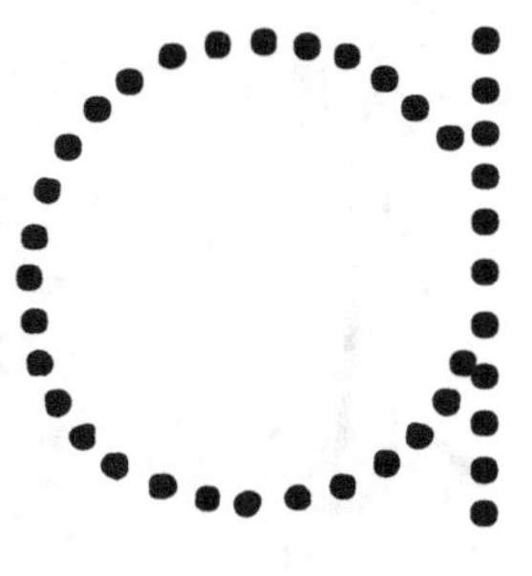

Trace the cursive letters, then write your own

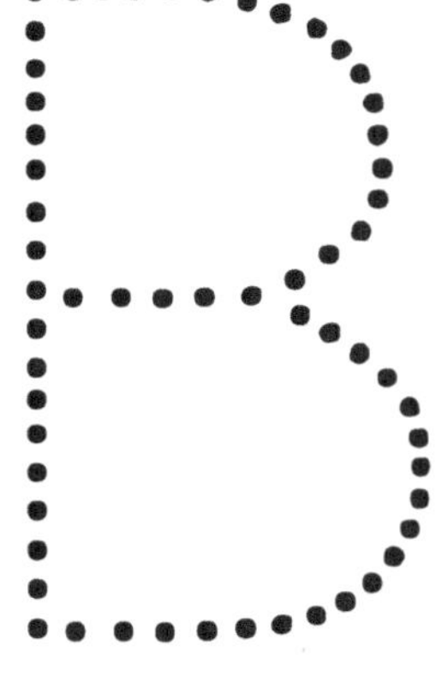

is for Banana

Trace the cursive letters, then write your own

b

is for banana

Trace the cursive letters, then write your own

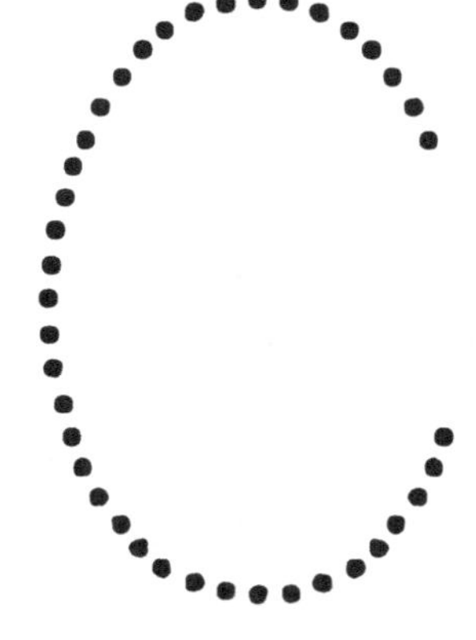

is for Car

Trace the cursive letters, then write your own

is for car

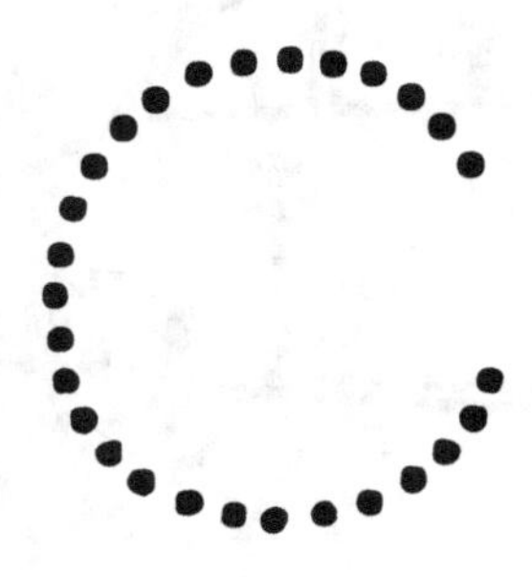

Trace the cursive letters, then write your own

is for Dog

Trace the cursive letters, then write your own

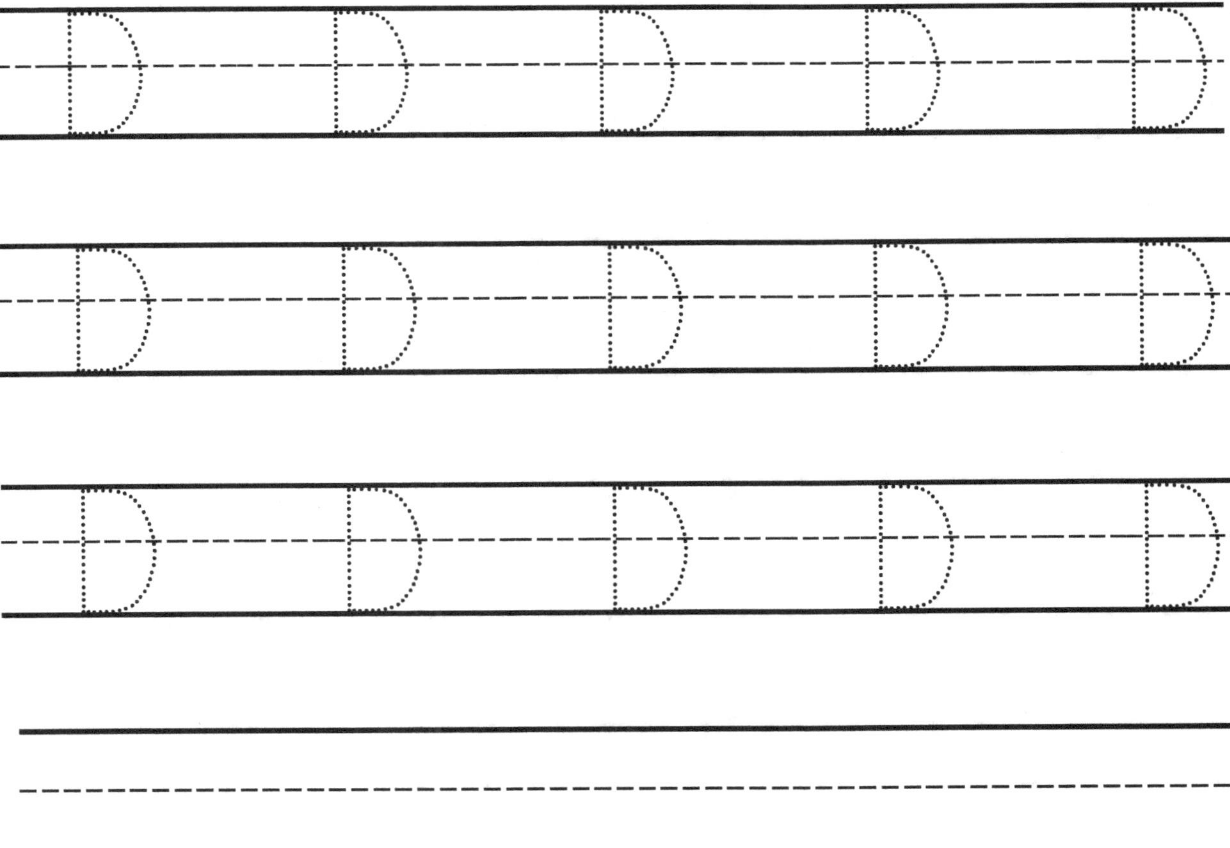

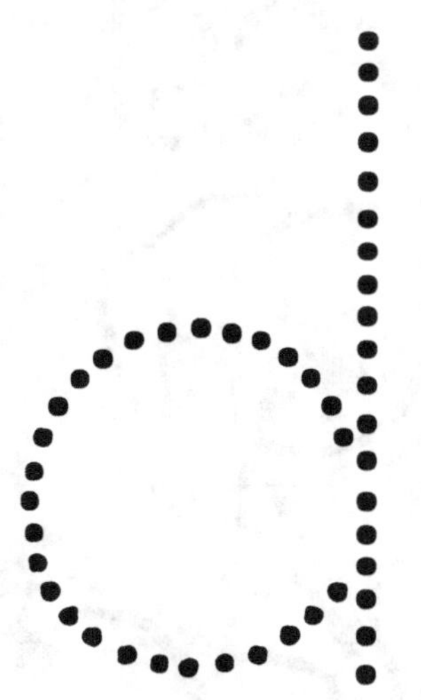

is for dog

Trace the cursive letters, then write your own

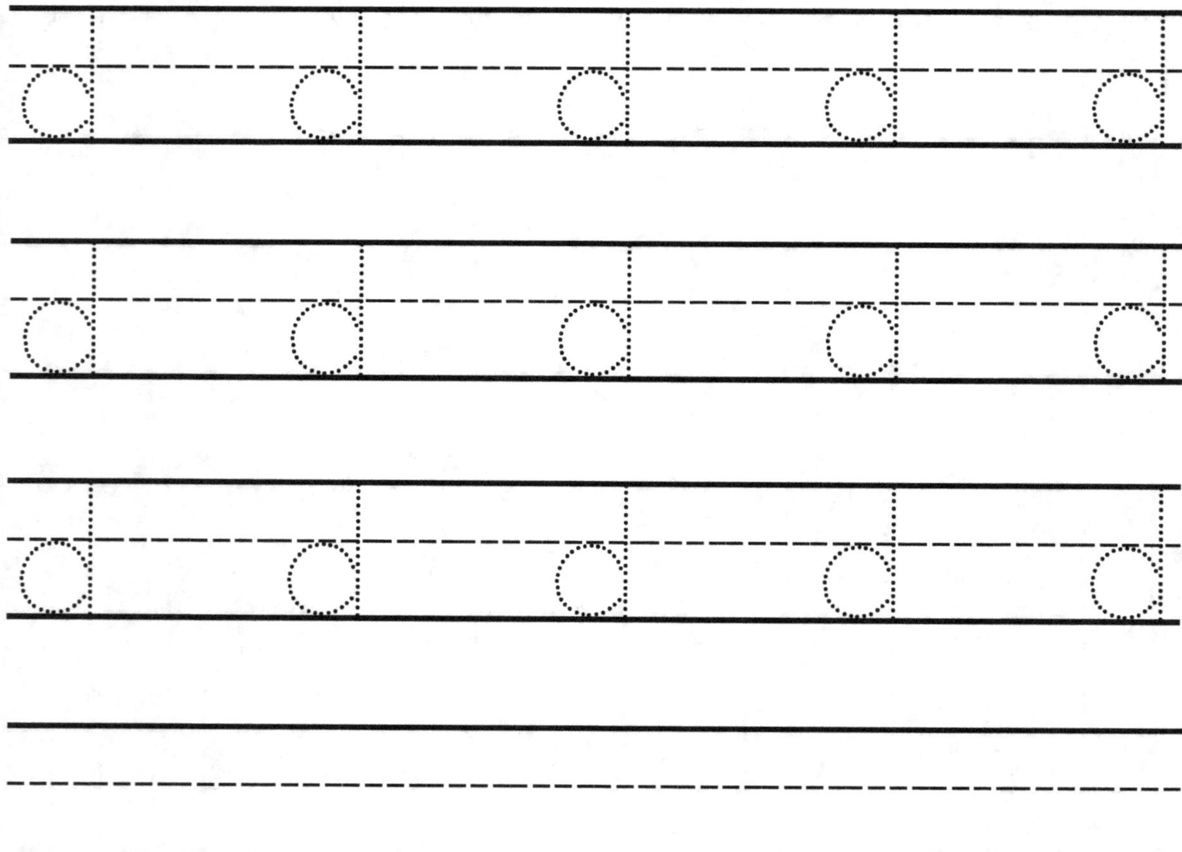

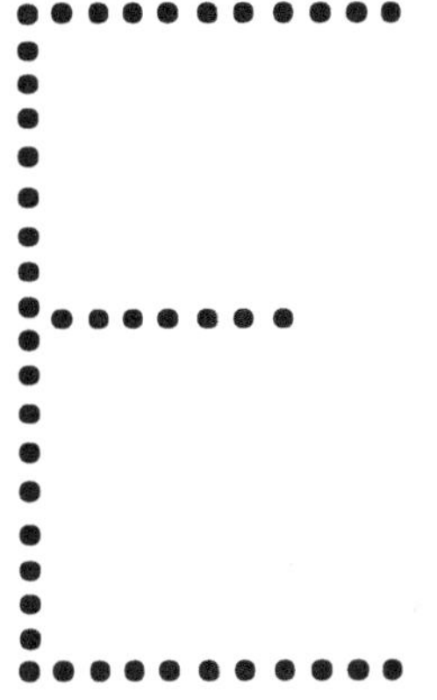

is for Elephant

Trace the cursive letters, then write your own

 is for elephant

Trace the cursive letters, then write your own

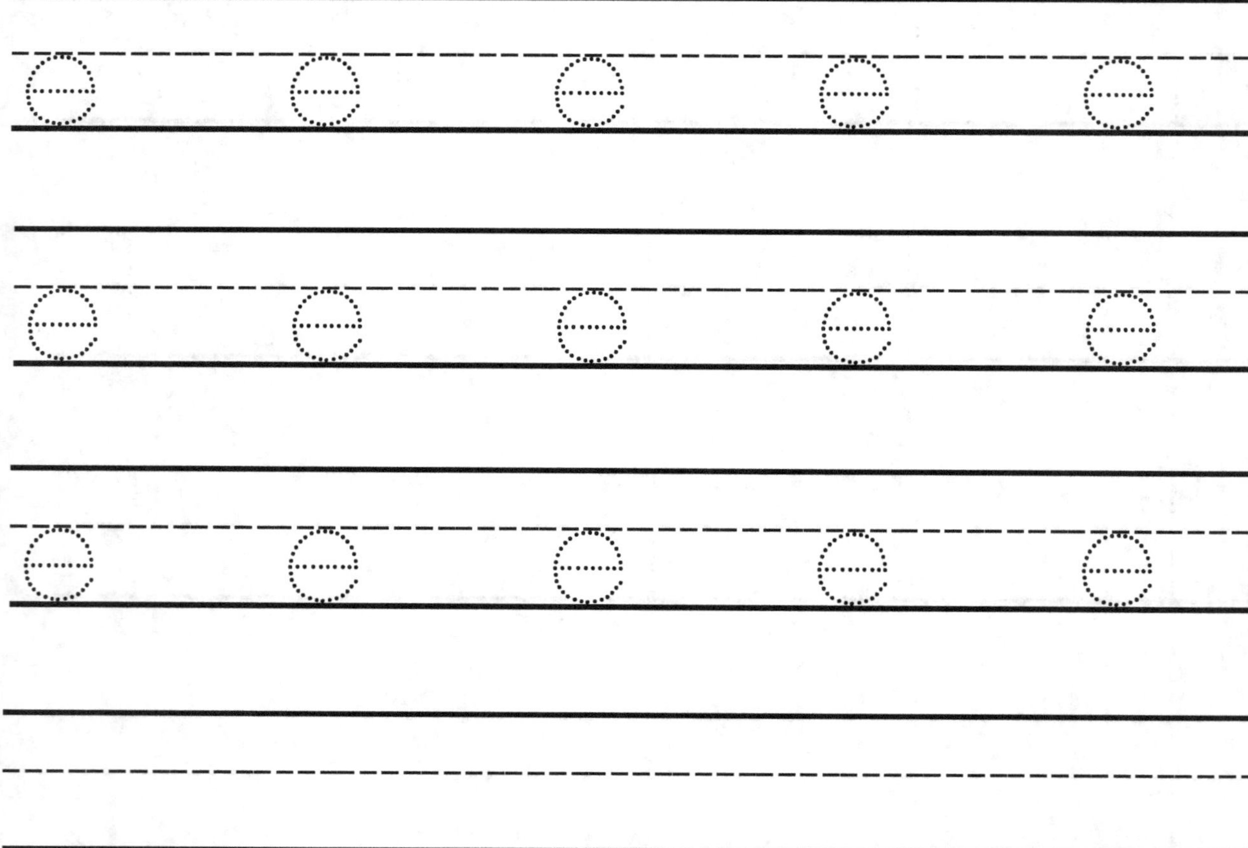

is for Fish

Trace the cursive letters, then write your own

is for fish

Trace the cursive letters, then write your own

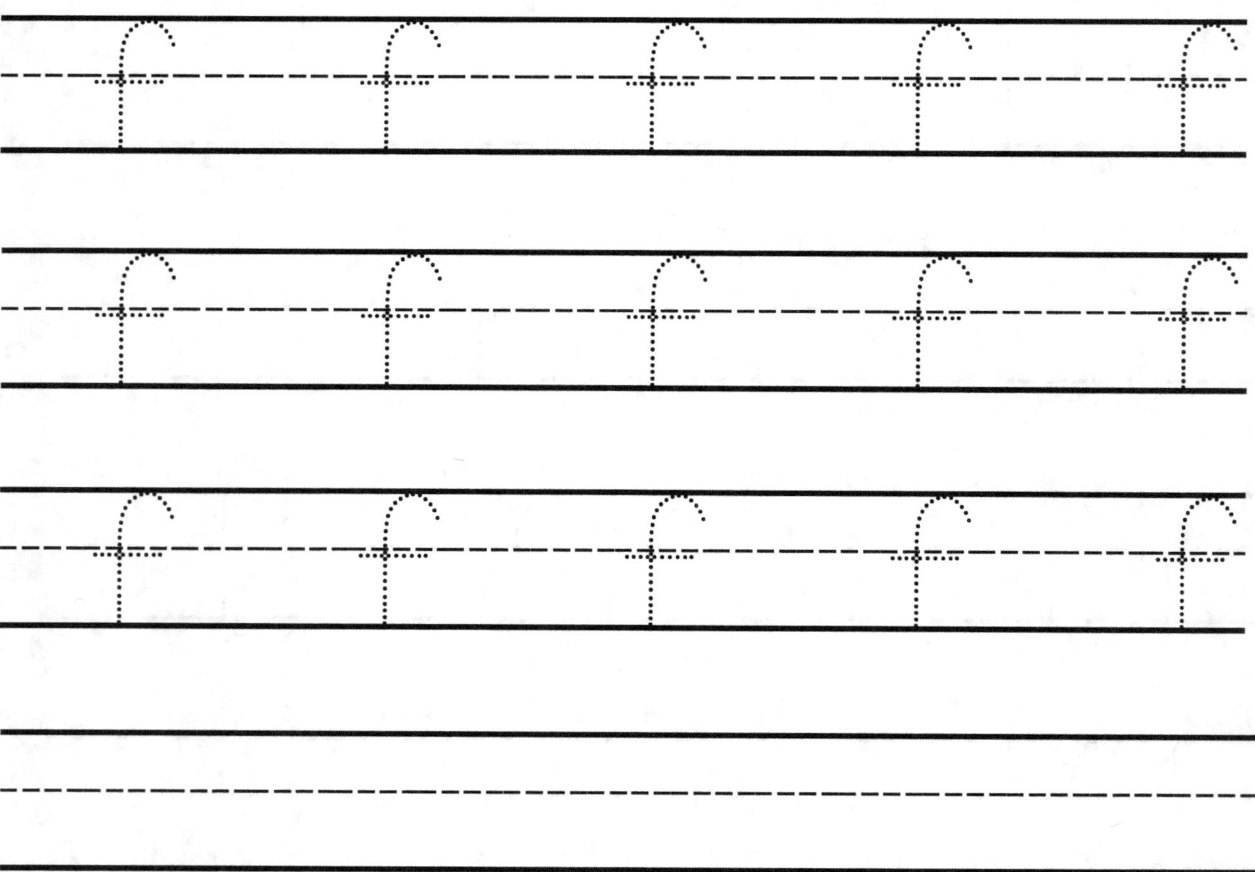

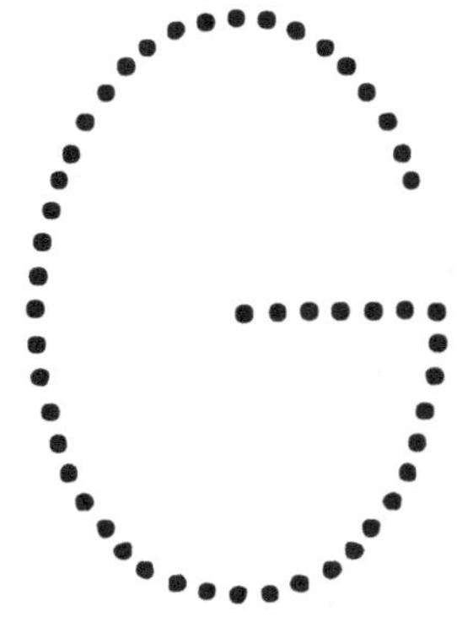

is for Grape

Trace the cursive letters, then write your own

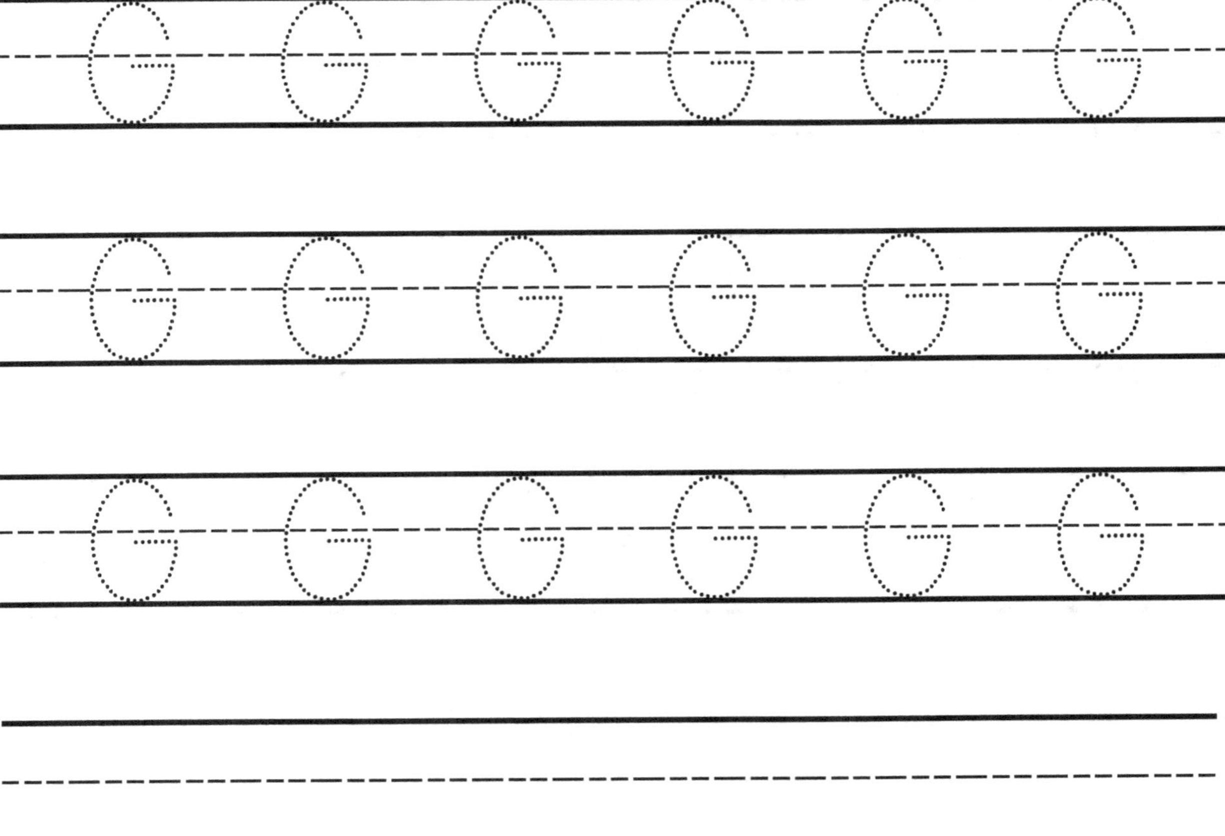

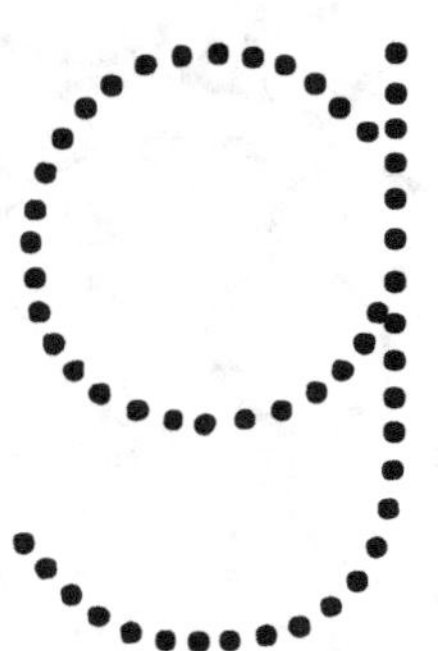

Trace the cursive letters, then write your own

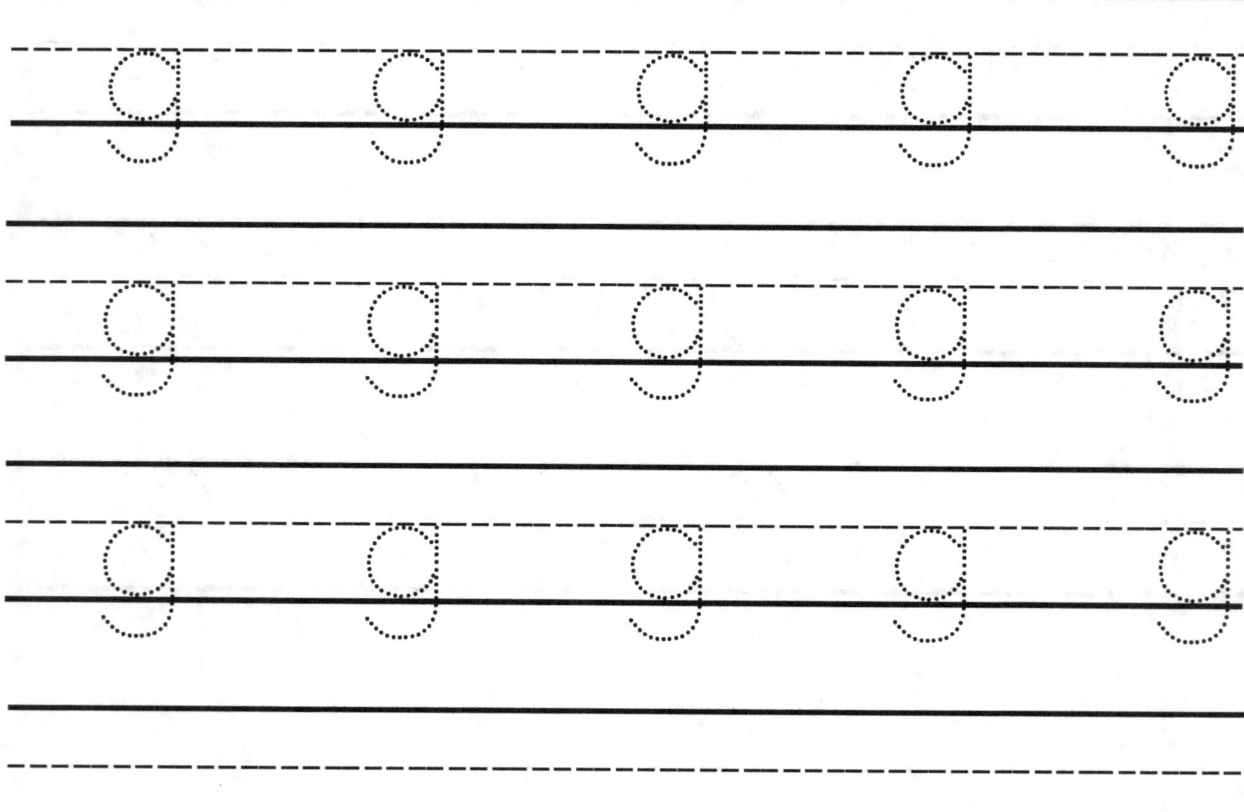

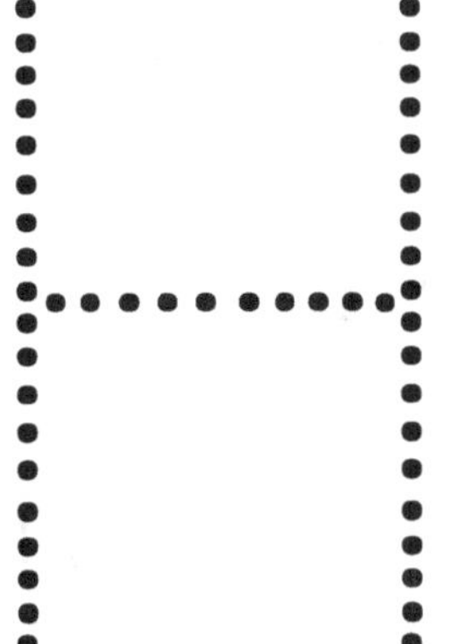

is for Hippo

Trace the cursive letters, then write your own

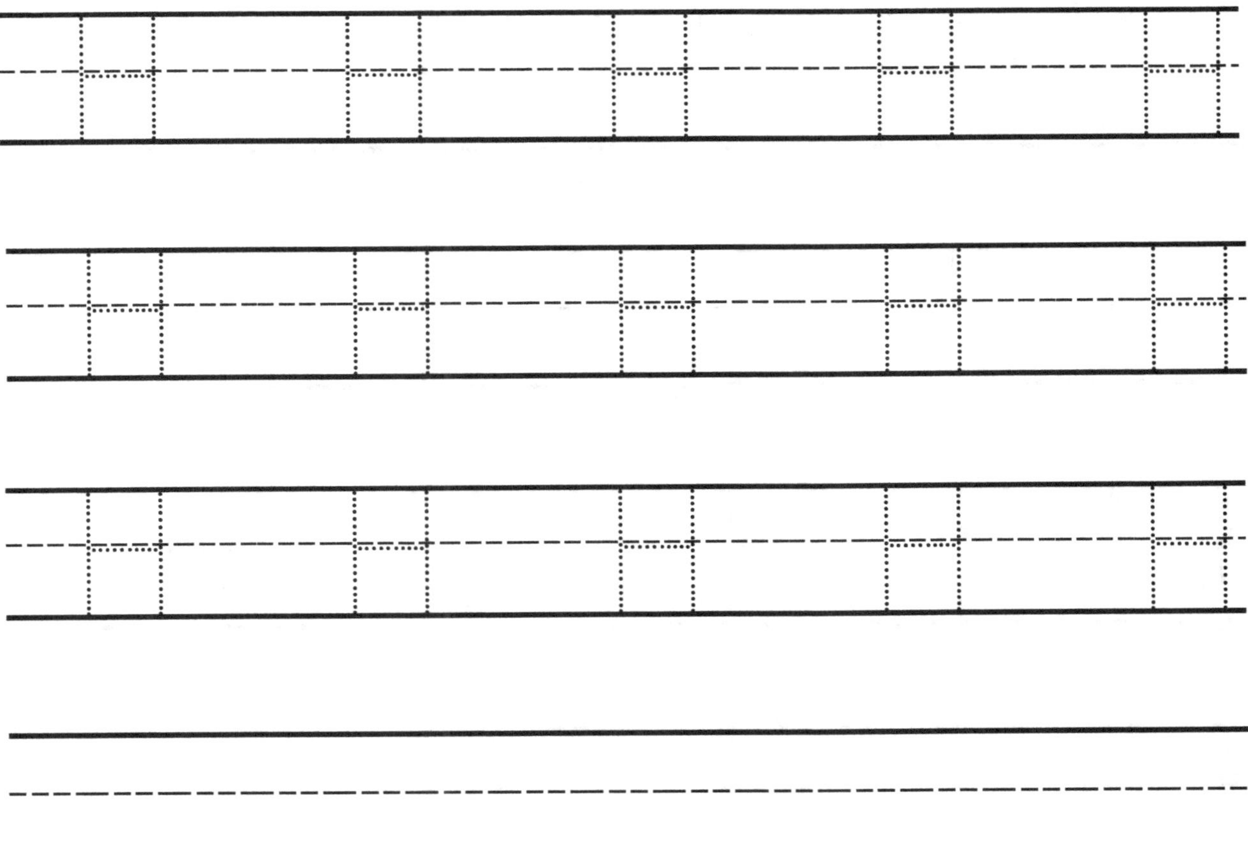

is for hippo

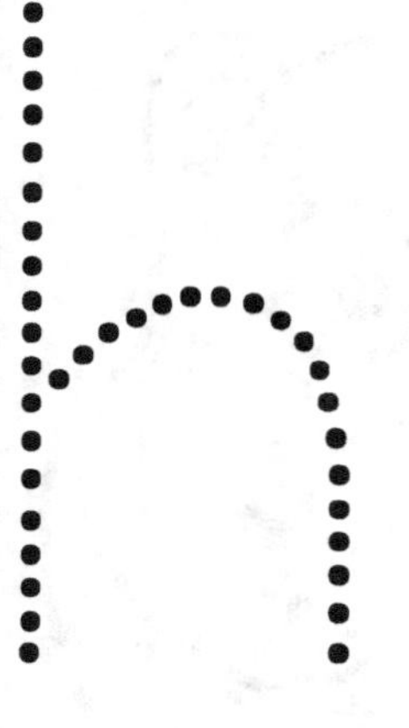

Trace the cursive letters, then write your own

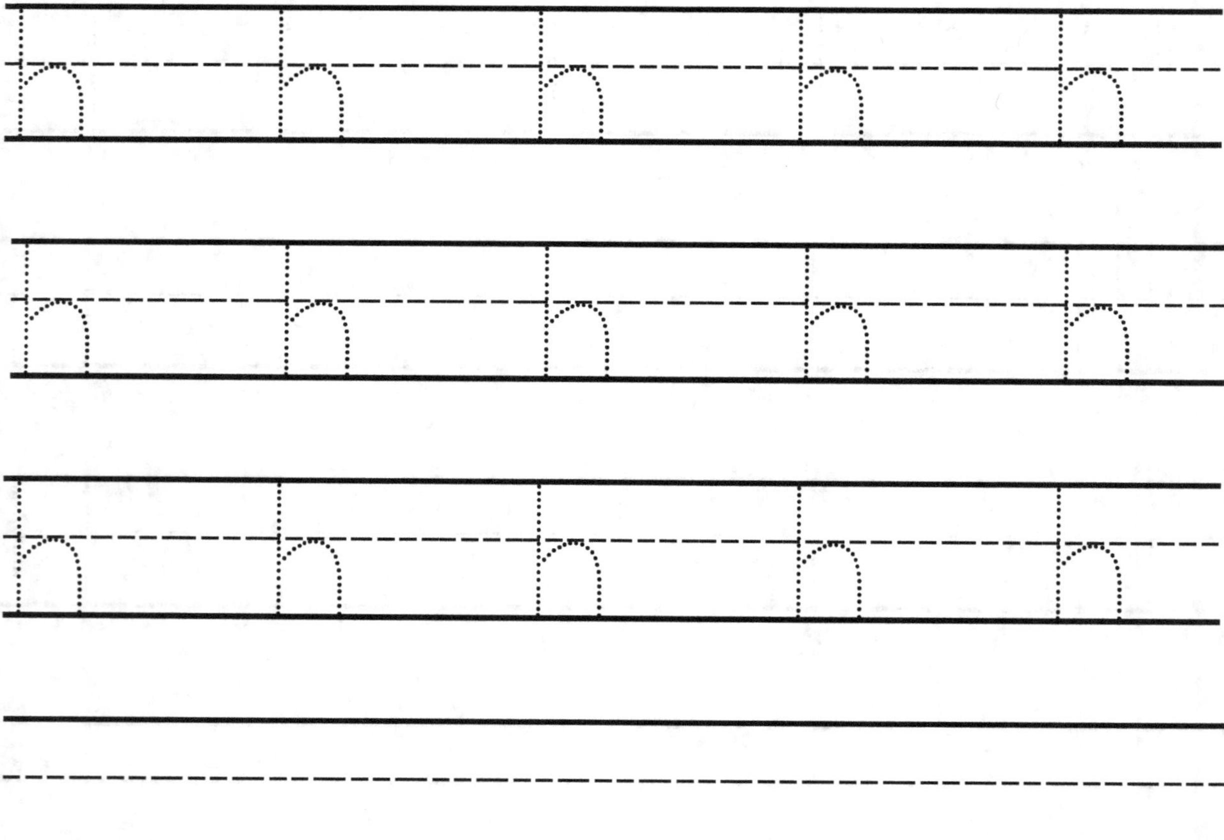

is for Ice Cream

Trace the cursive letters, then write your own

is for Ice cream

Trace the cursive letters, then write your own

J is for Jellyfish

Trace the cursive letters, then write your own

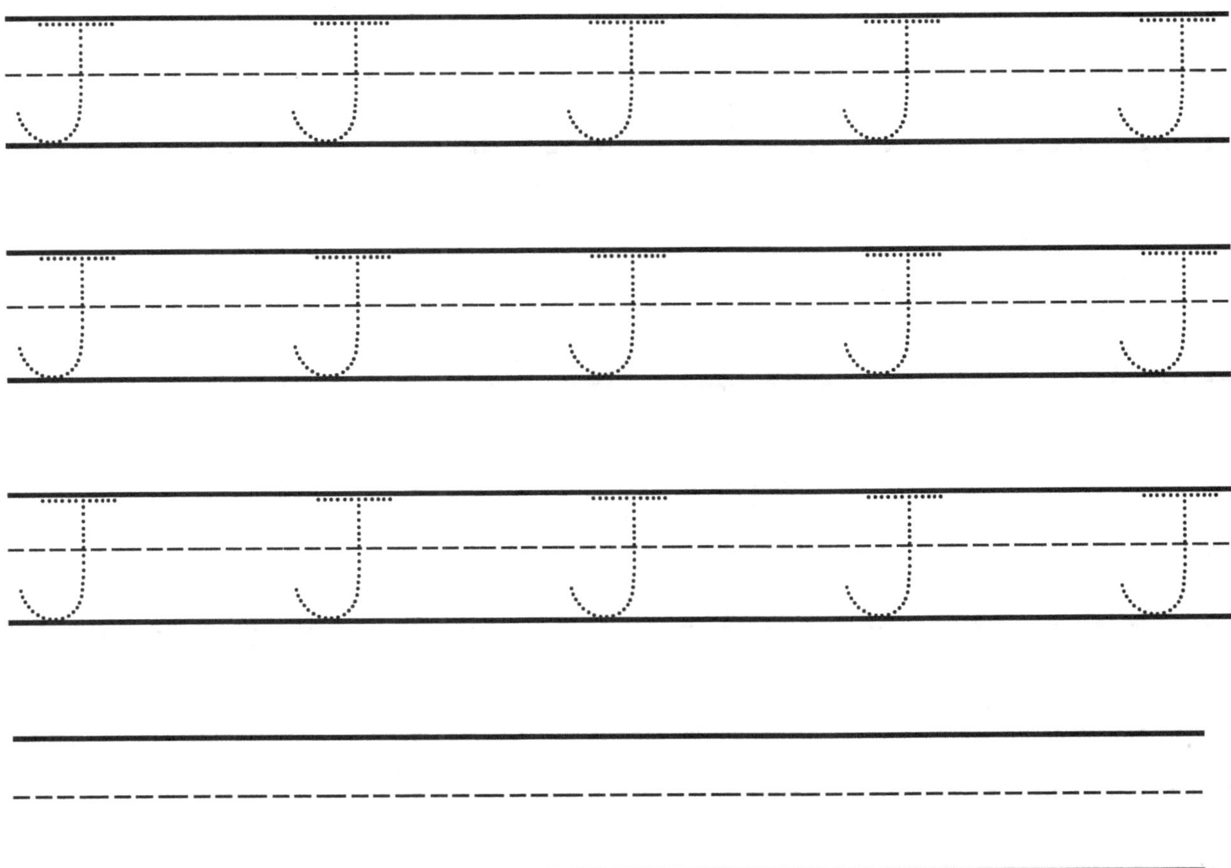

is for jellyfish

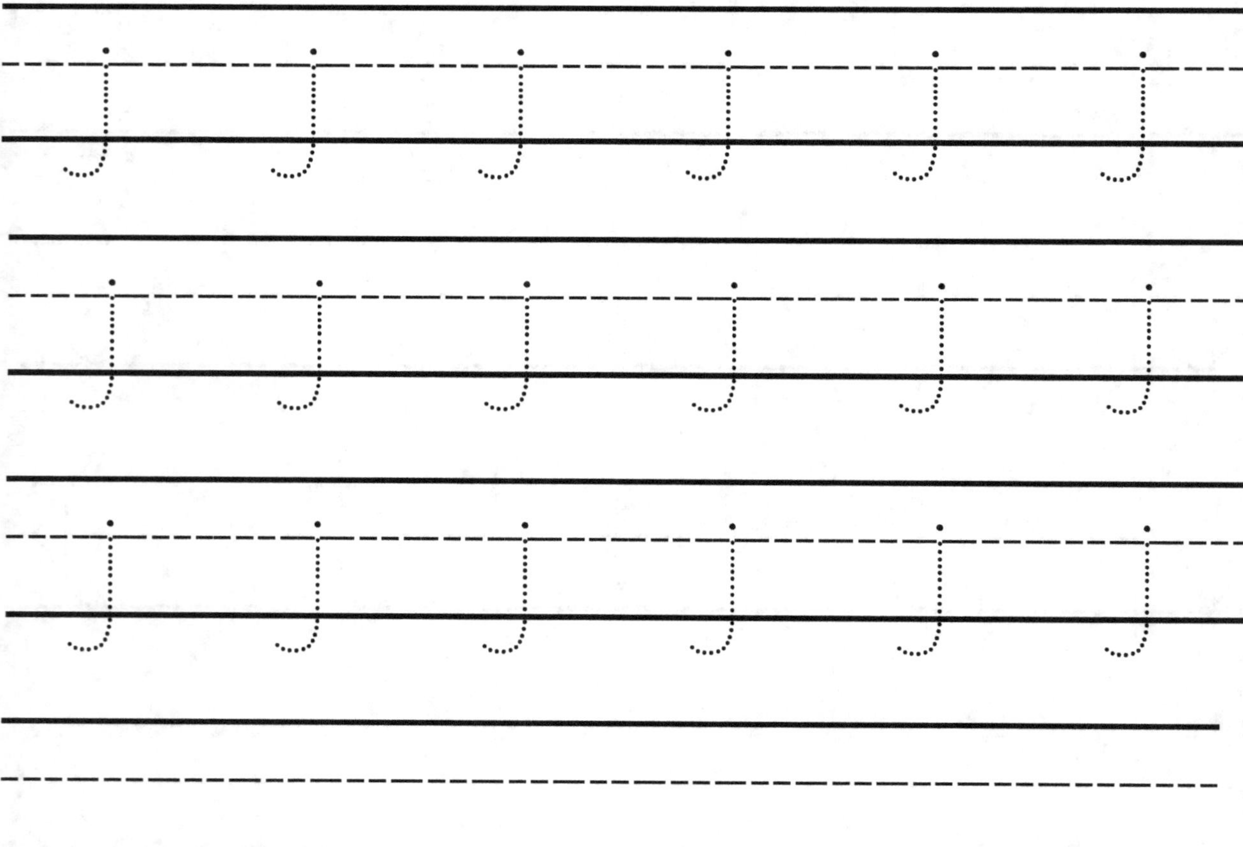

Trace the cursive letters, then write your own

Trace the cursive letters, then write your own

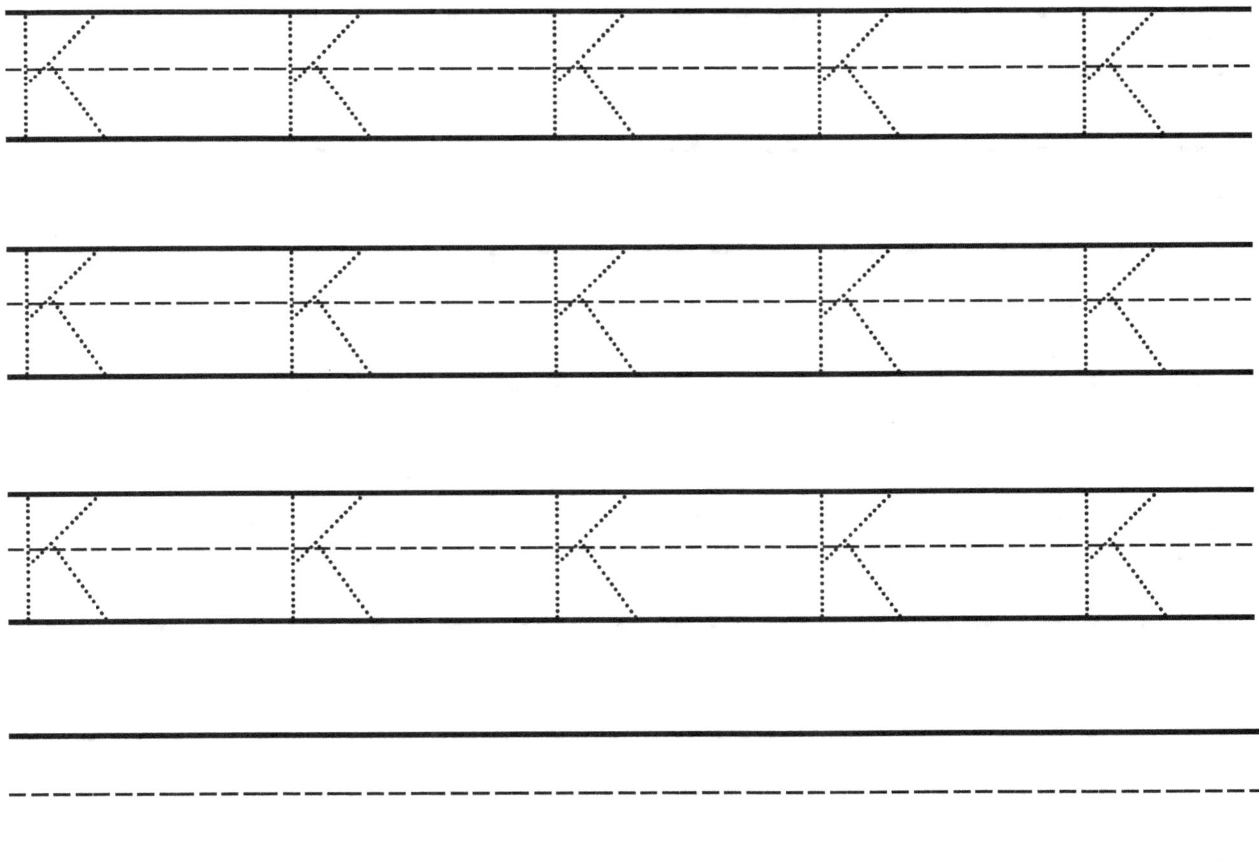

is for koala

Trace the cursive letters, then write your own

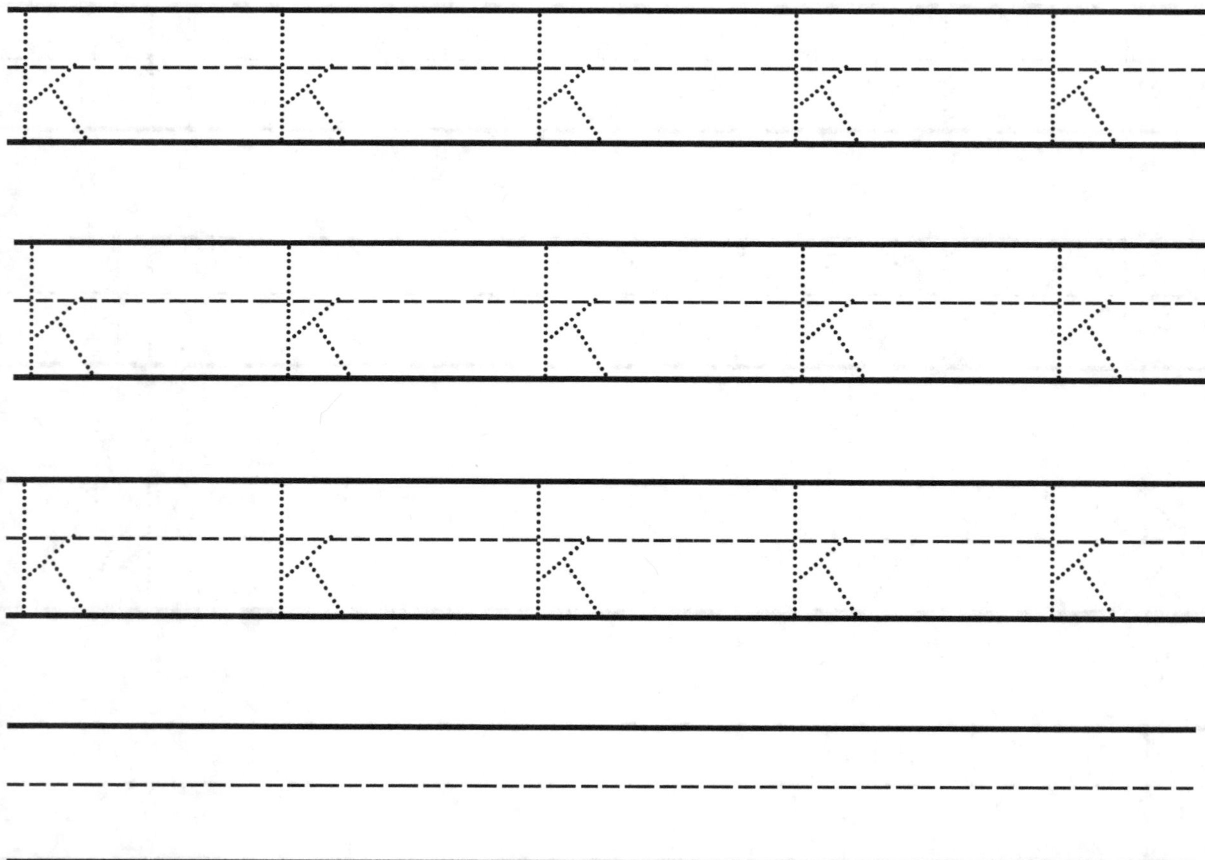

is for Ladybird

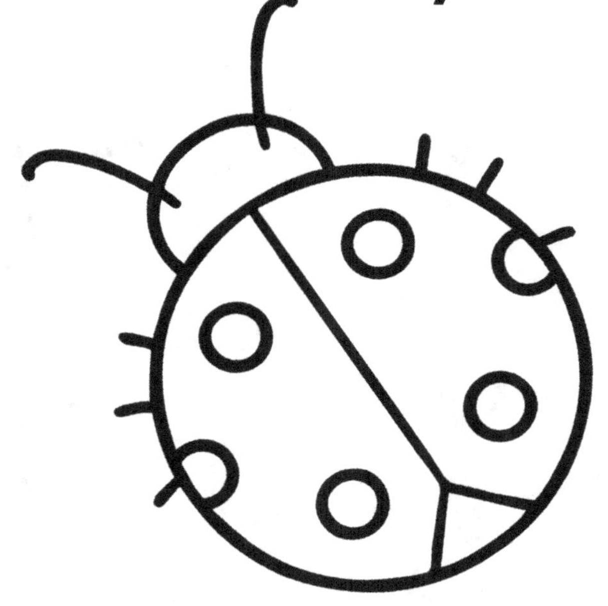

Trace the cursive letters, then write your own

is for Ladybird

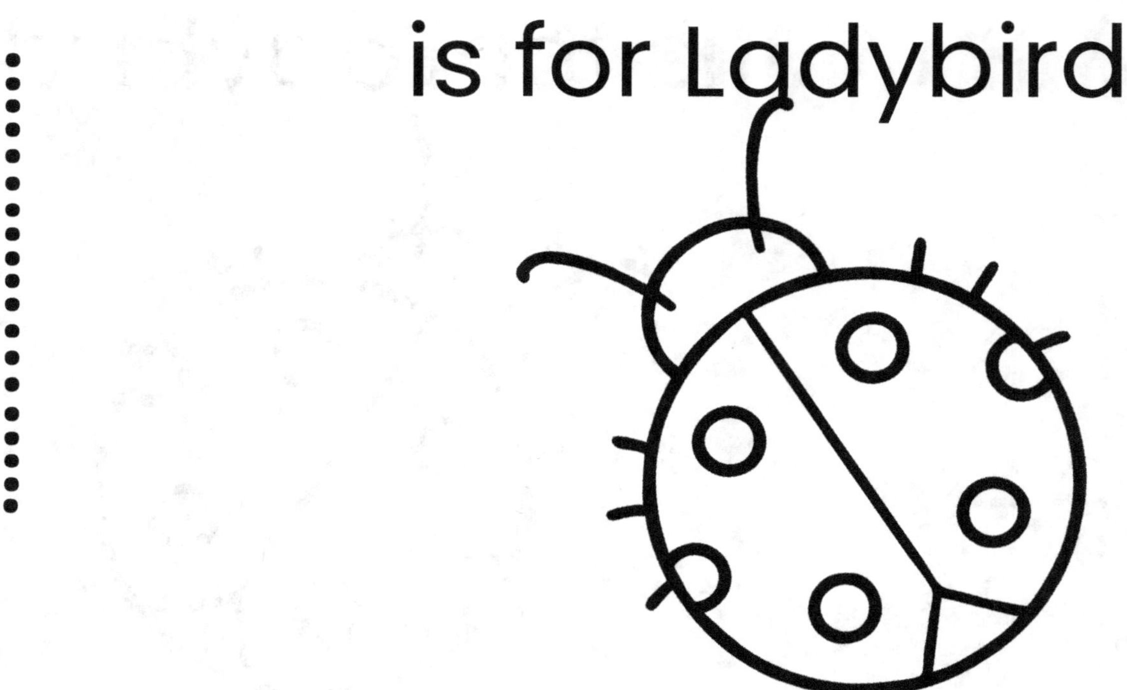

Trace the cursive letters, then write your own

is for Mouse

Trace the cursive letters, then write your own

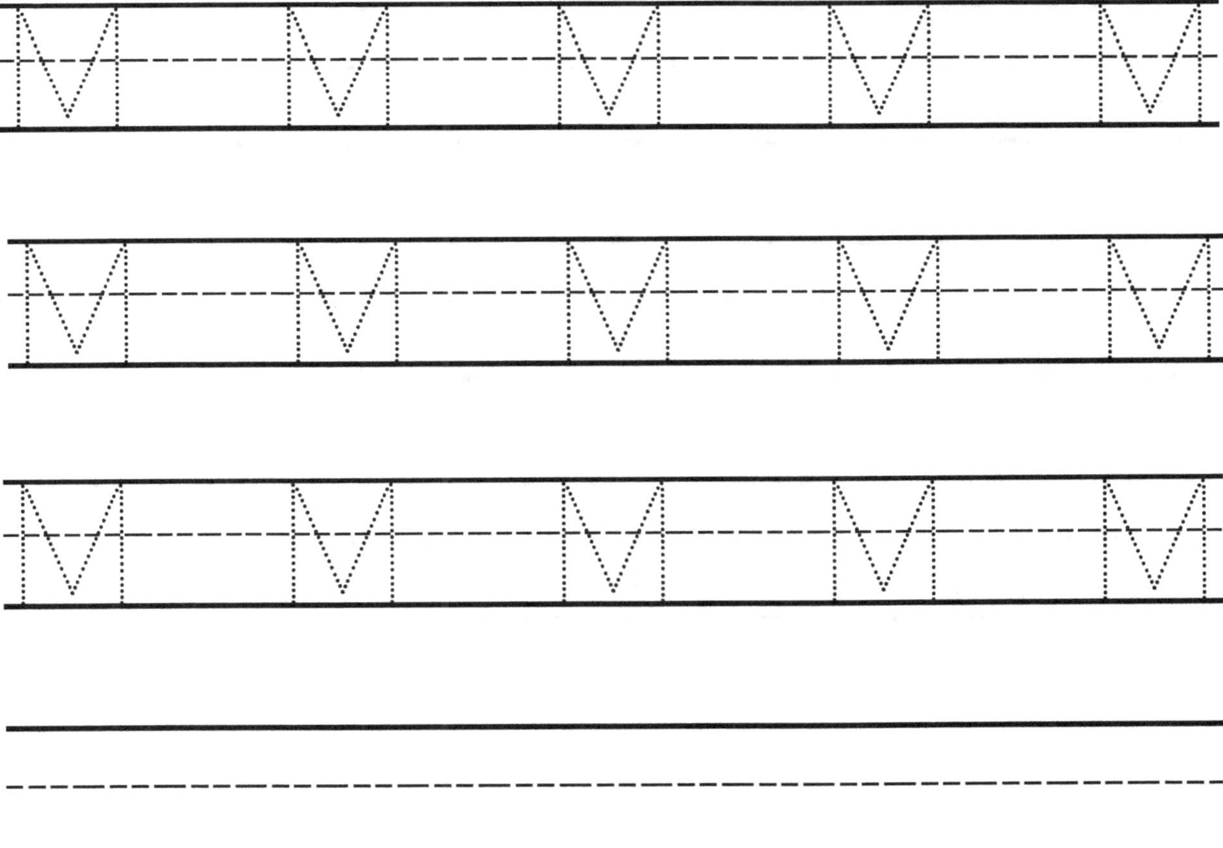

is for mouse

Trace the cursive letters, then write your own

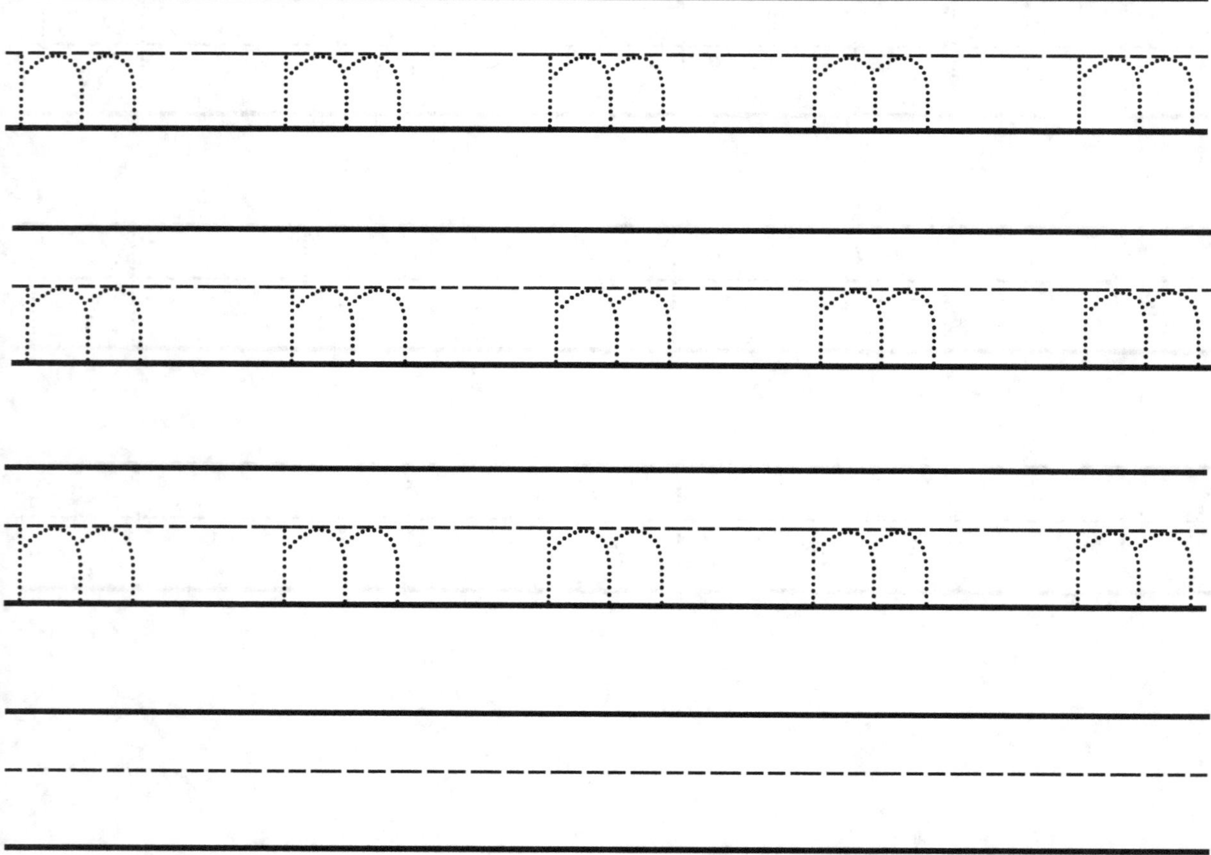

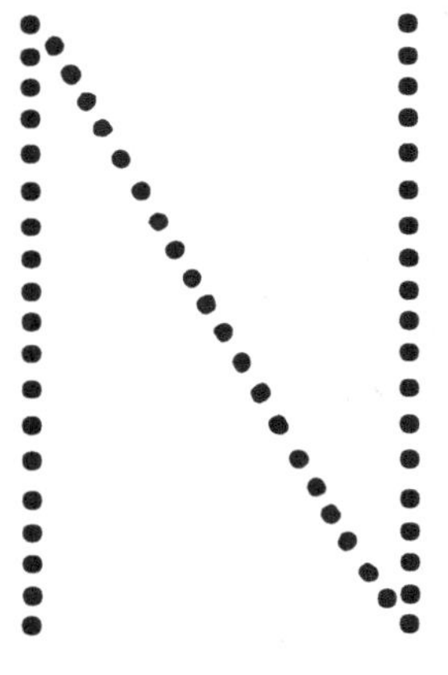

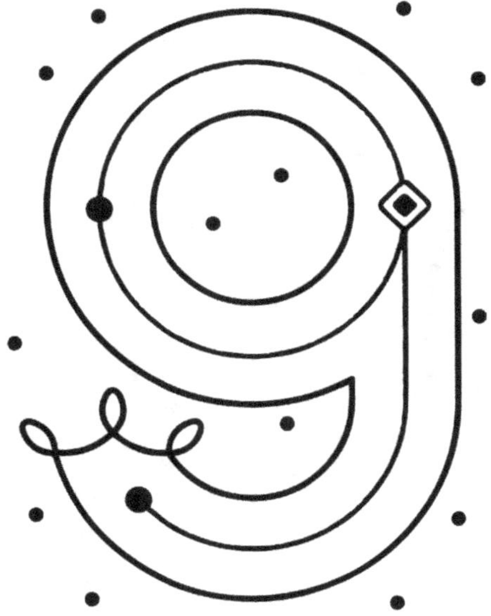

is for Nine

Trace the cursive letters, then write your own

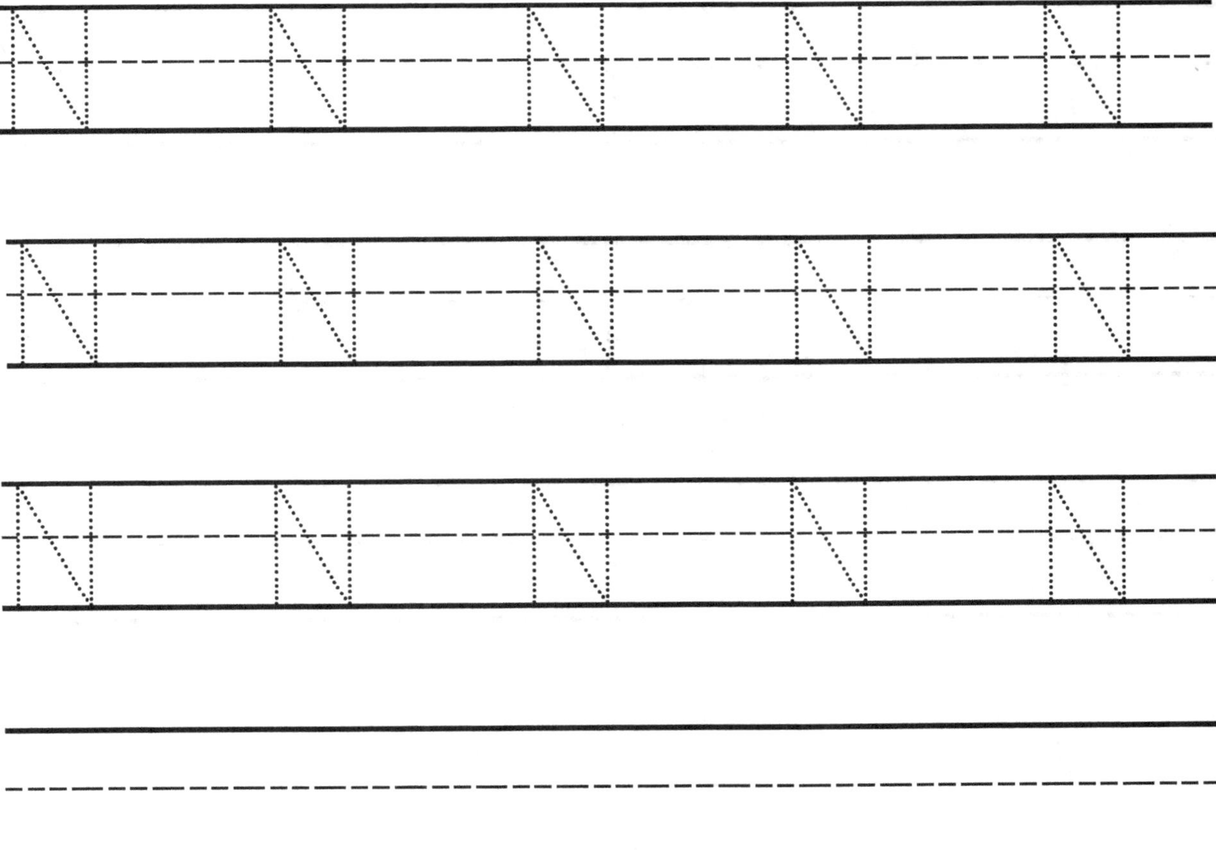

is for nine

Trace the cursive letters, then write your own

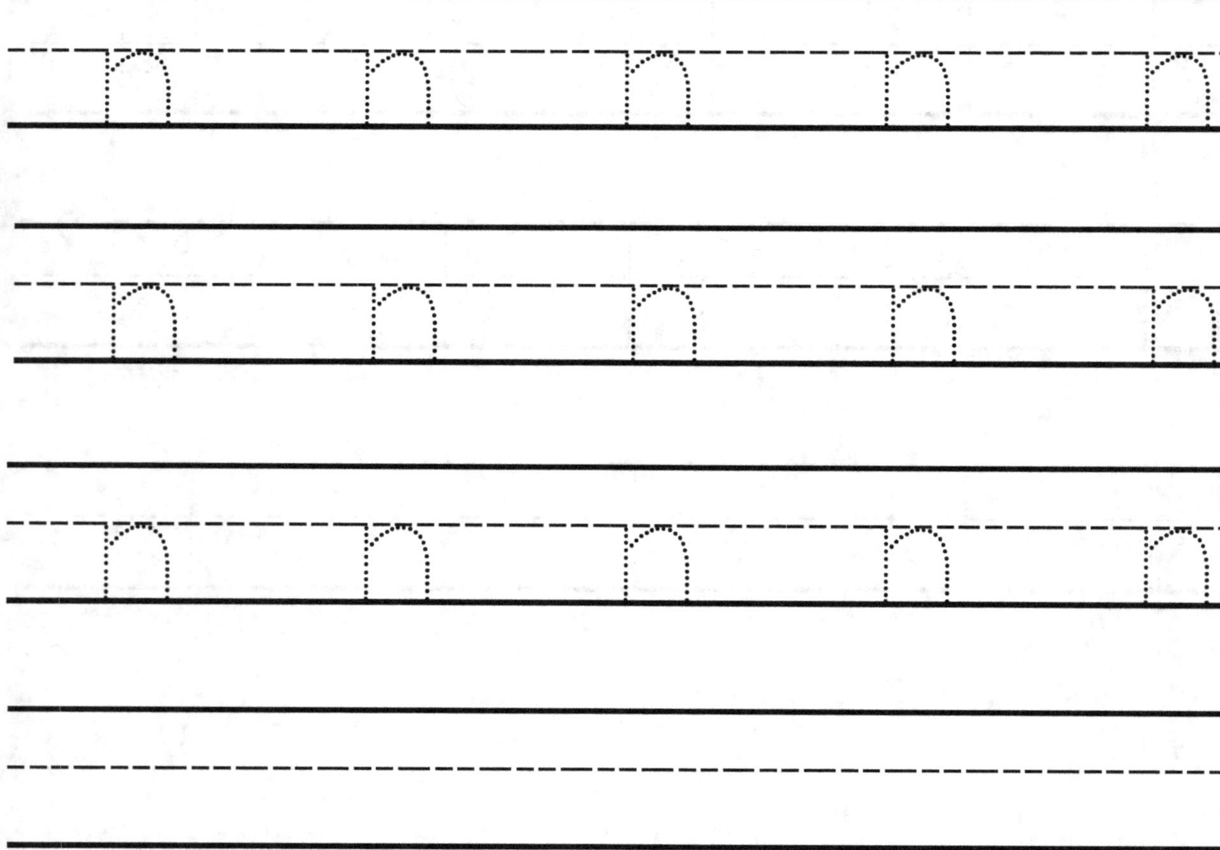

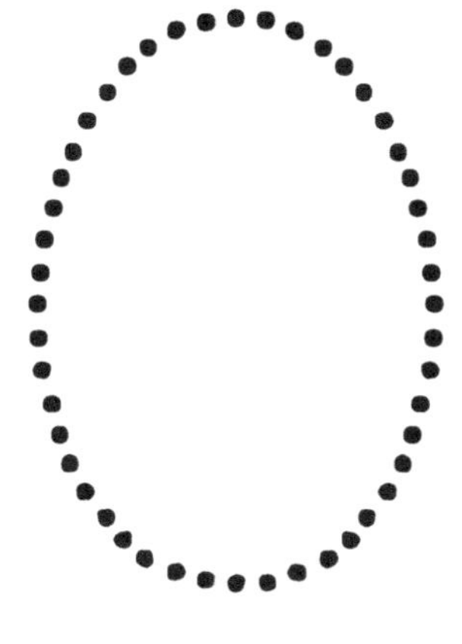

is for Onion

Trace the cursive letters, then write your own

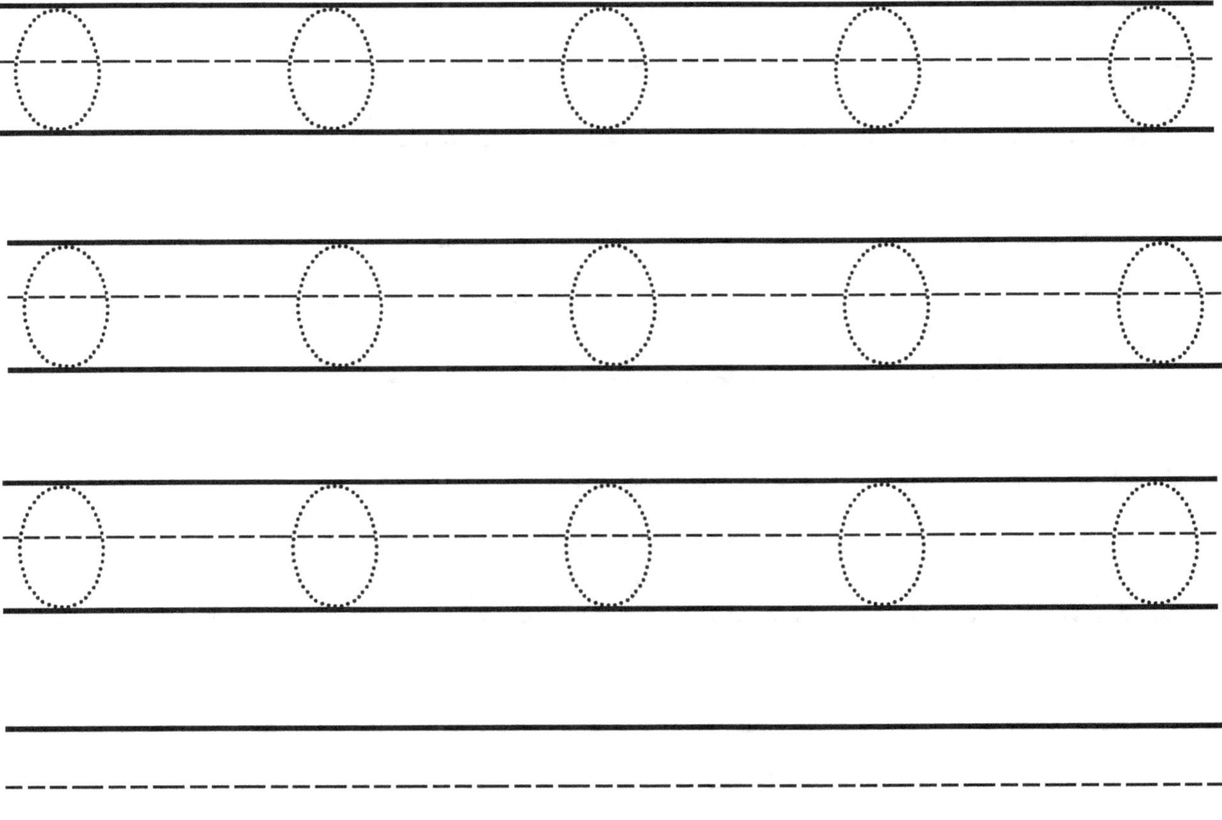

is for onion

Trace the cursive letters, then write your own

P

is for Popcorn

Trace the cursive letters, then write your own

is for popcorn

Trace the cursive letters, then write your own

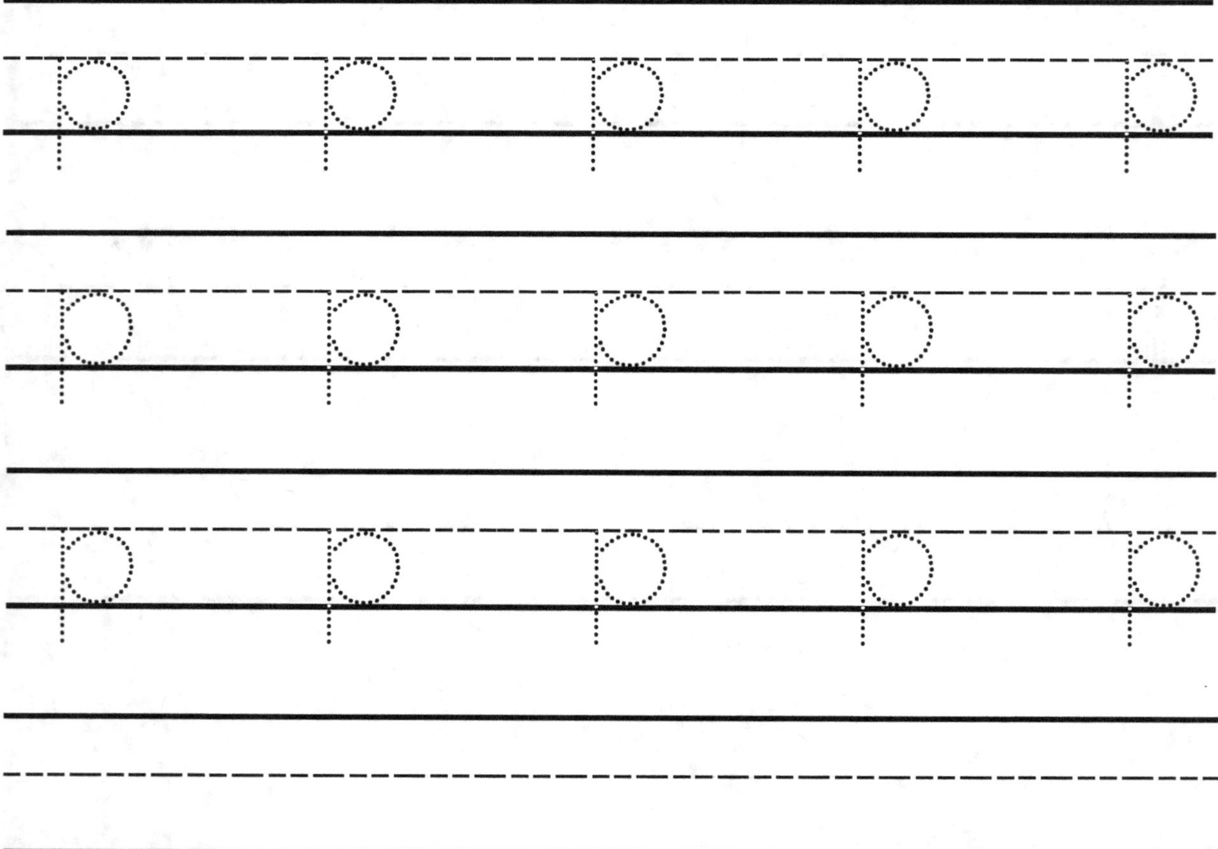

Trace the cursive letters, then write your own

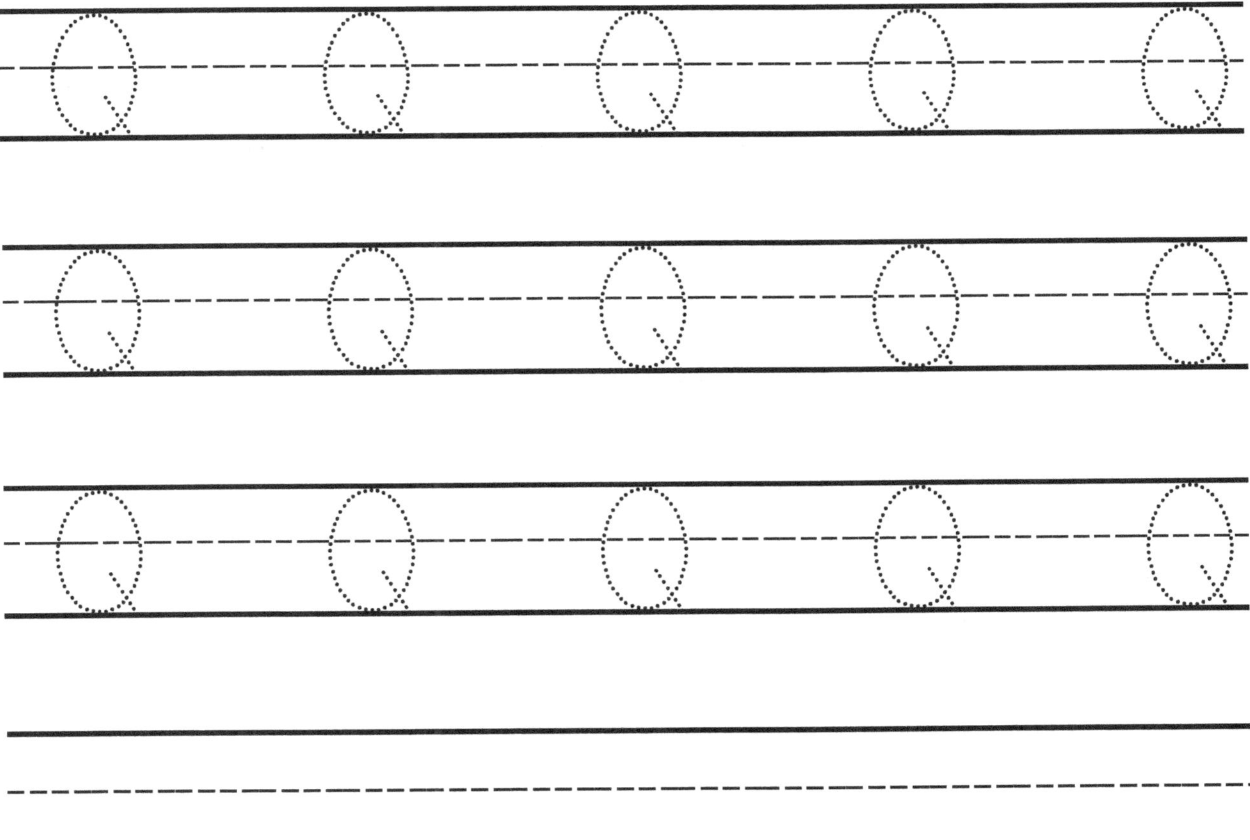

is for queen

Trace the cursive letters, then write your own

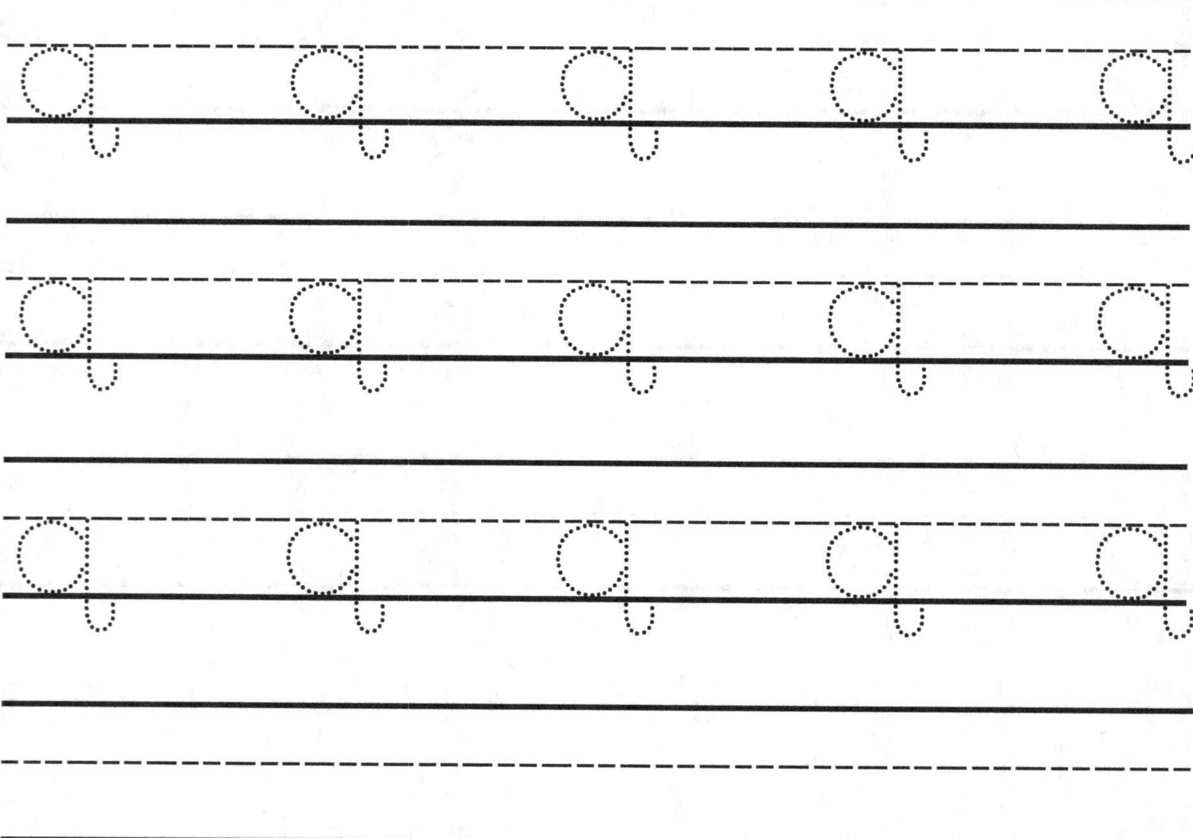

R is for Rabbit

Trace the cursive letters, then write your own

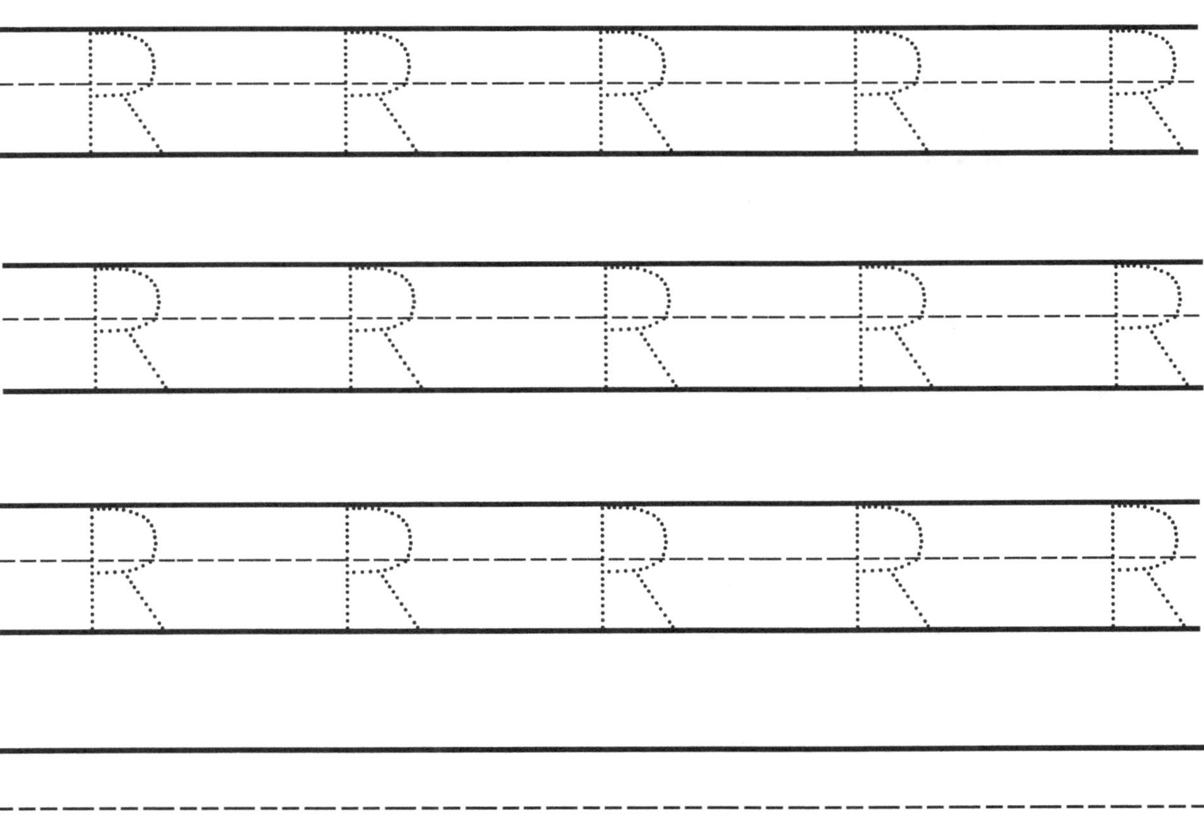

is for rabbit

Trace the cursive letters, then write your own

is for Strawberry

Trace the cursive letters, then write your own

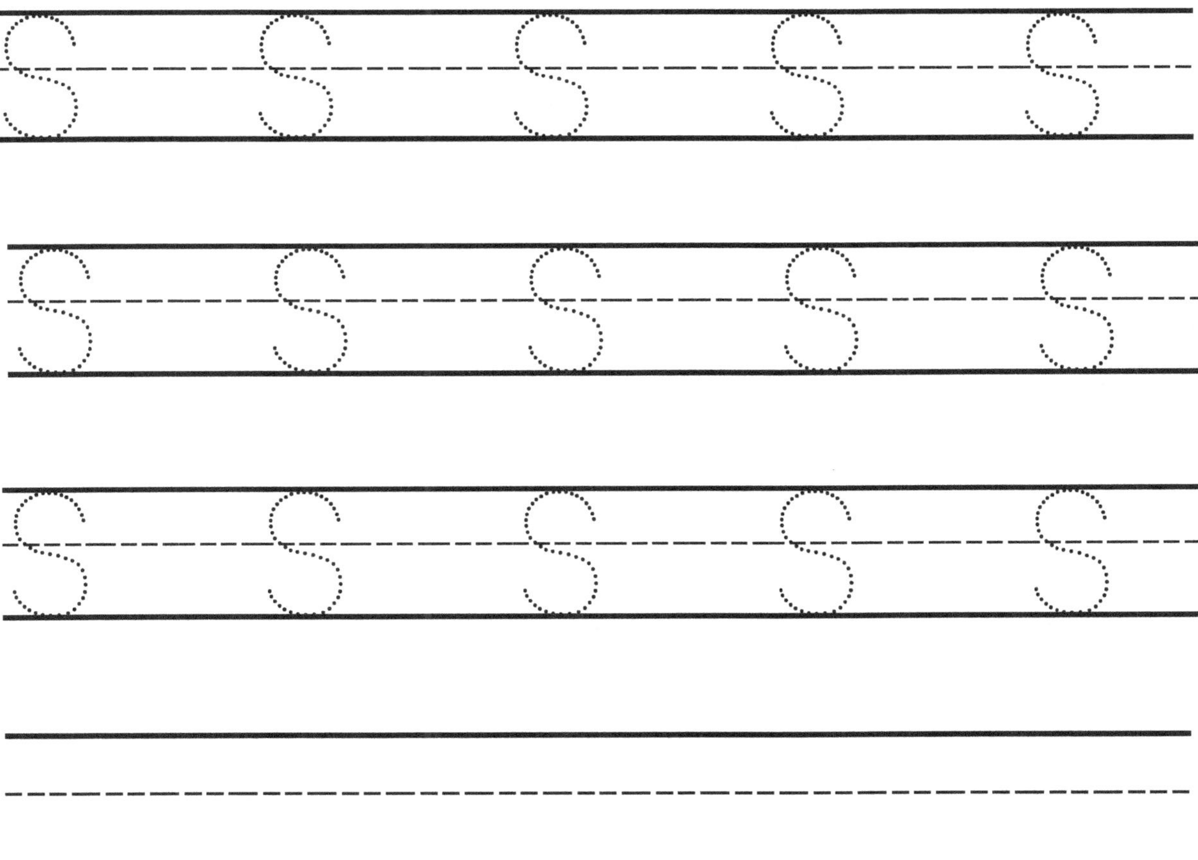

is for strawberry

Trace the cursive letters, then write your own

T is for Teddy

Trace the cursive letters, then write your own

Trace the cursive letters, then write your own

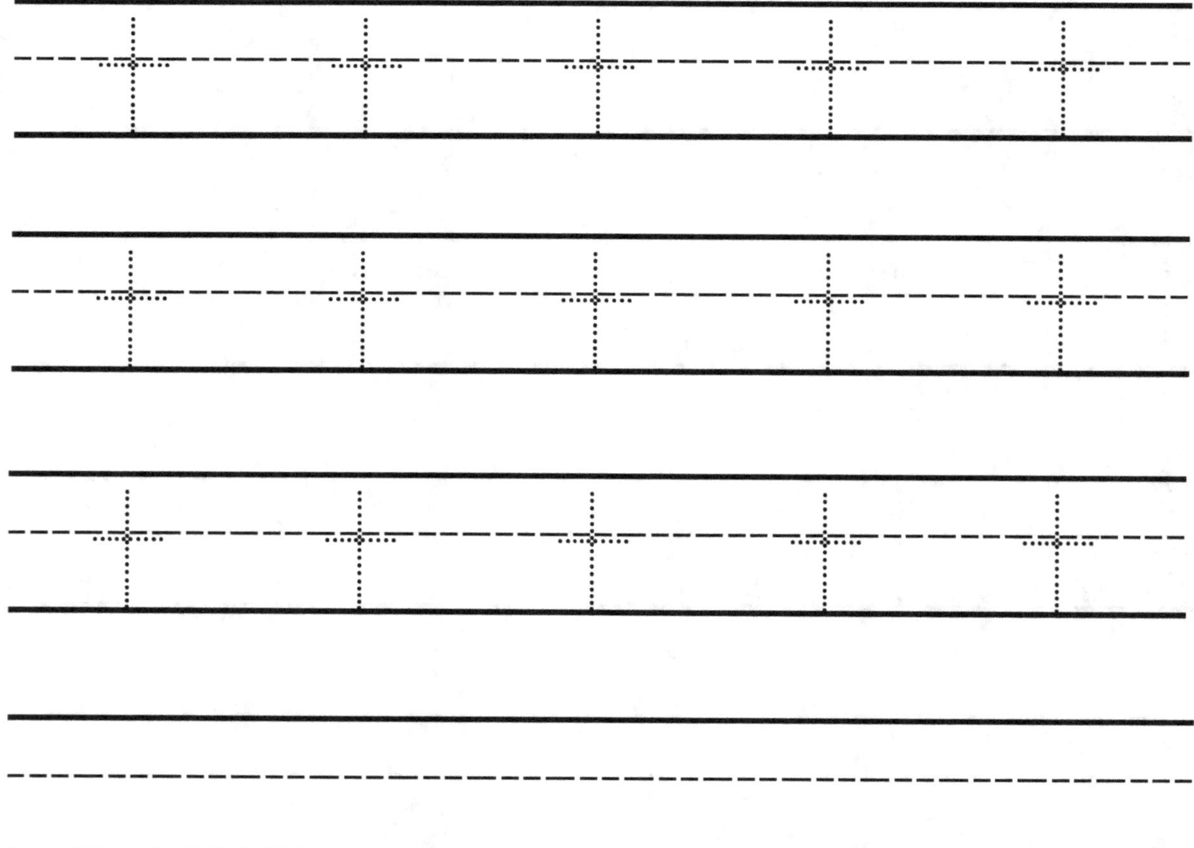

is for Umbrella

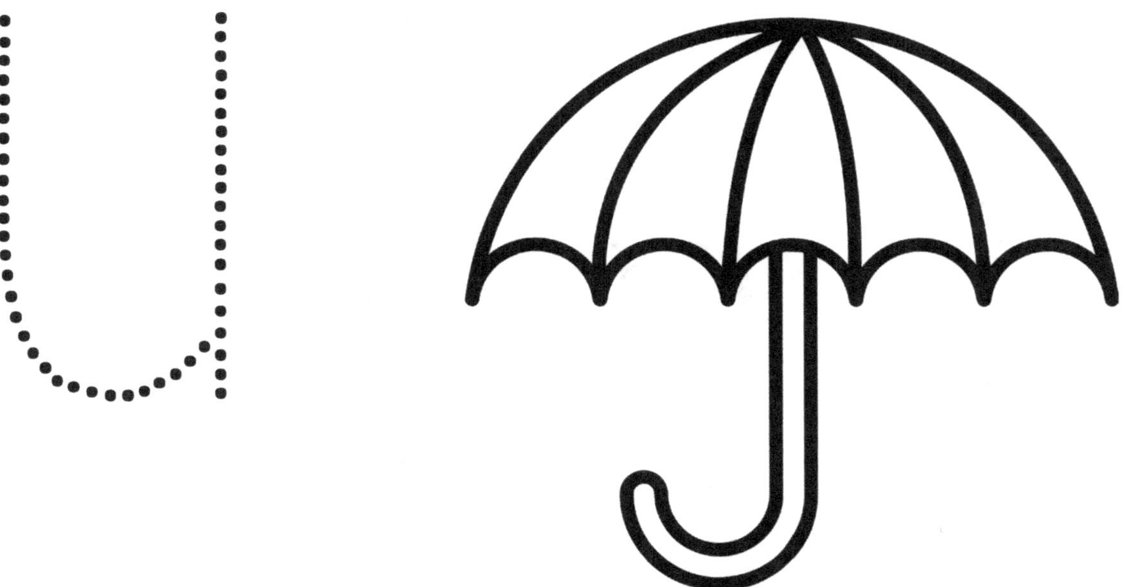

Trace the cursive letters, then write your own

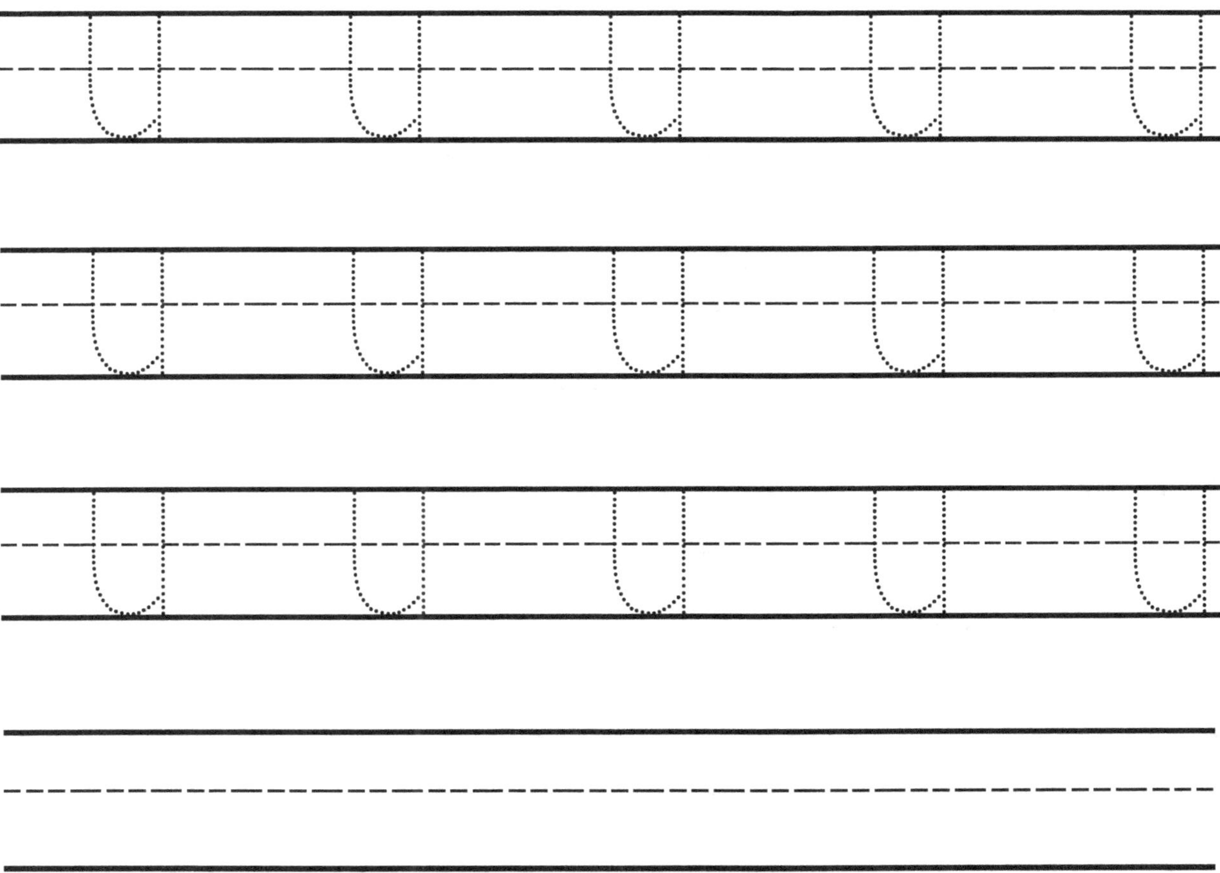

is for umbrella

Trace the cursive letters, then write your own

is for Volleyball

Trace the cursive letters, then write your own

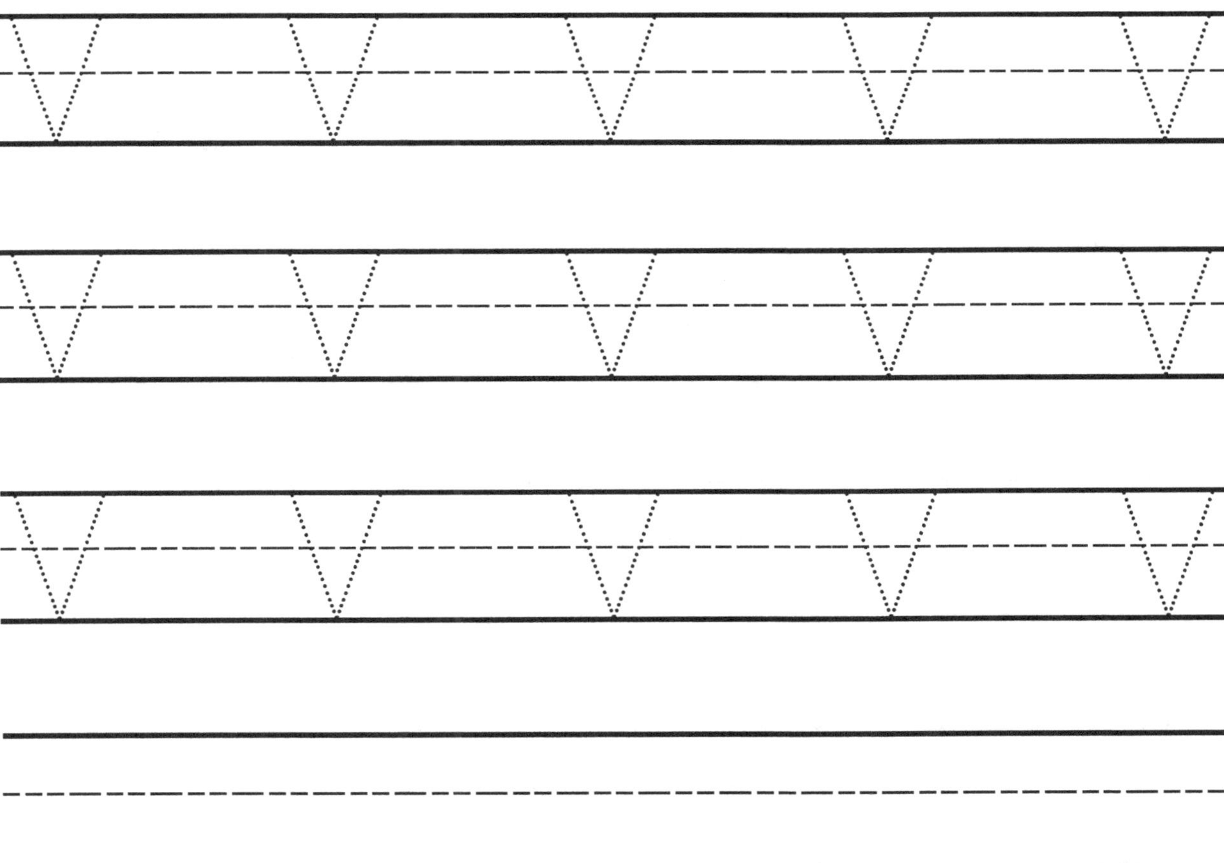

is for volleyball

Trace the cursive letters, then write your own

is for Watermelon

Trace the cursive letters, then write your own

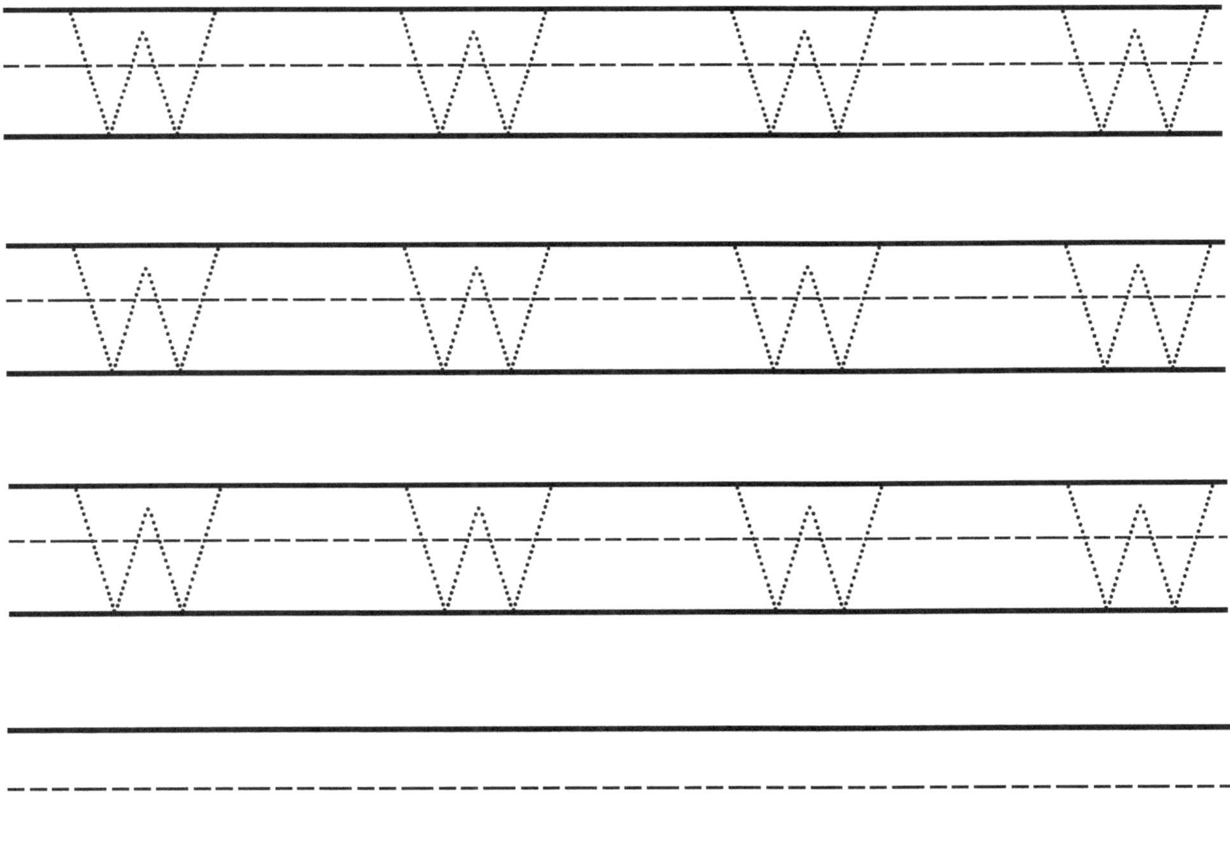

is for watermelon

Trace the cursive letters, then write your own

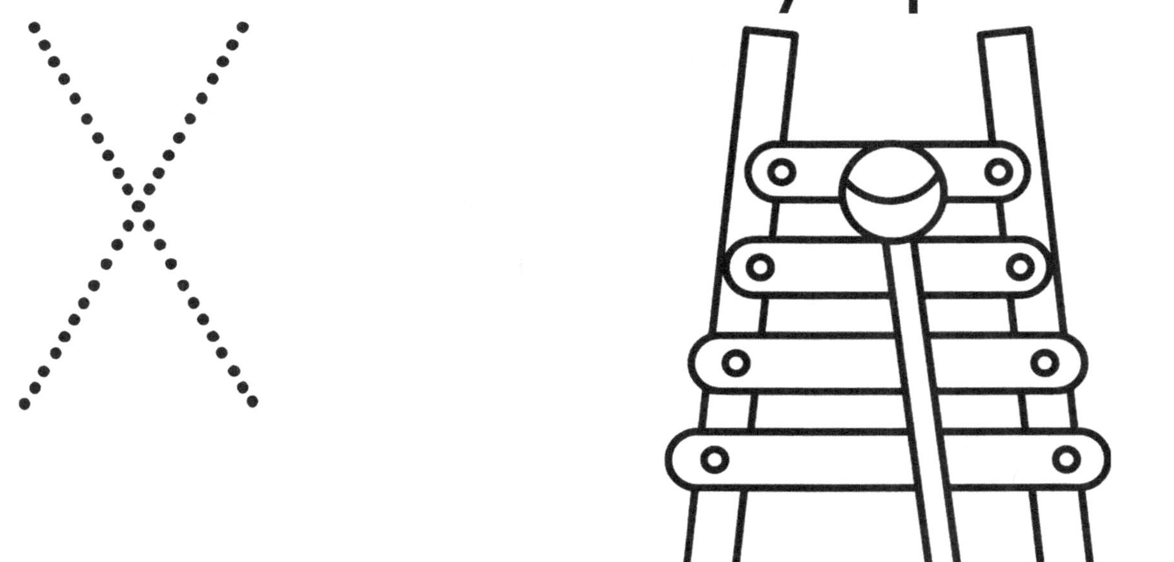

is for Xylophone

Trace the cursive letters, then write your own

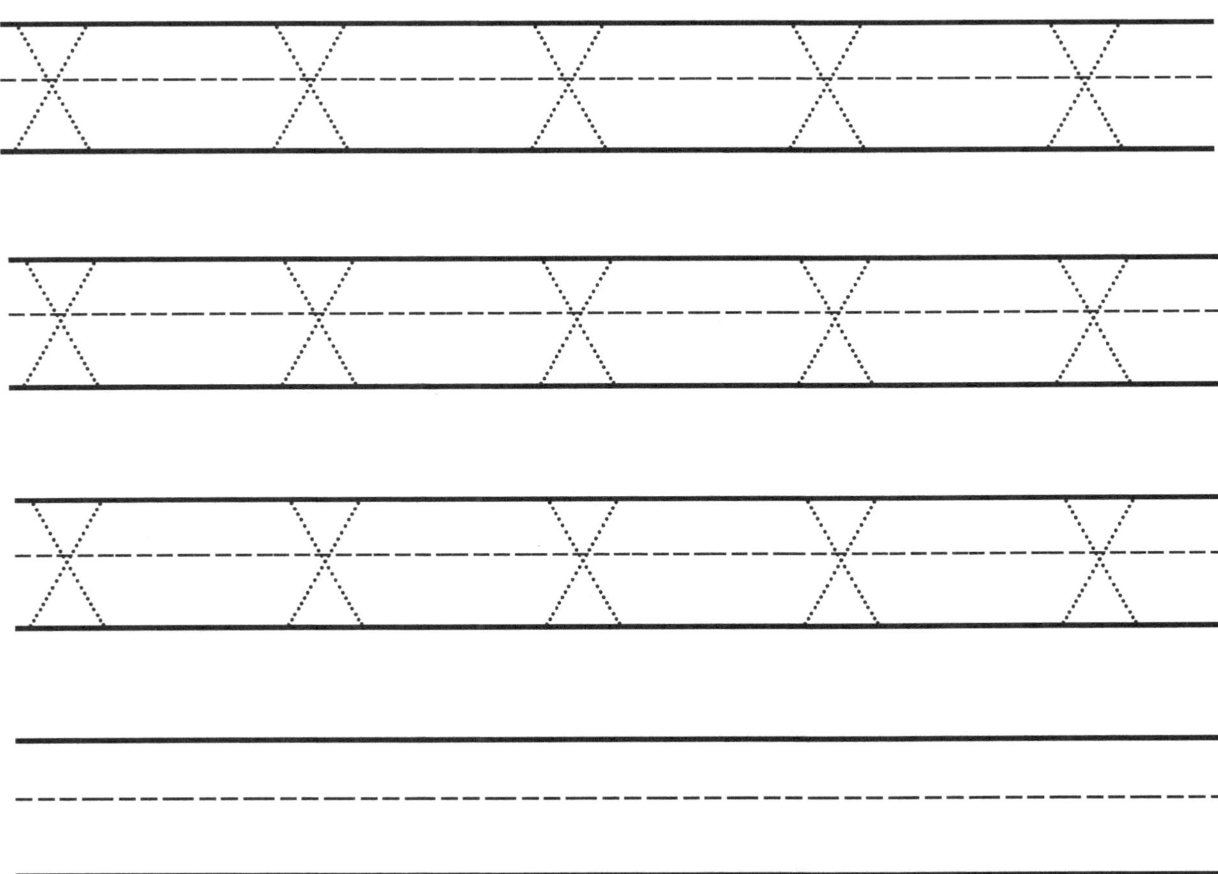

is for xylophone

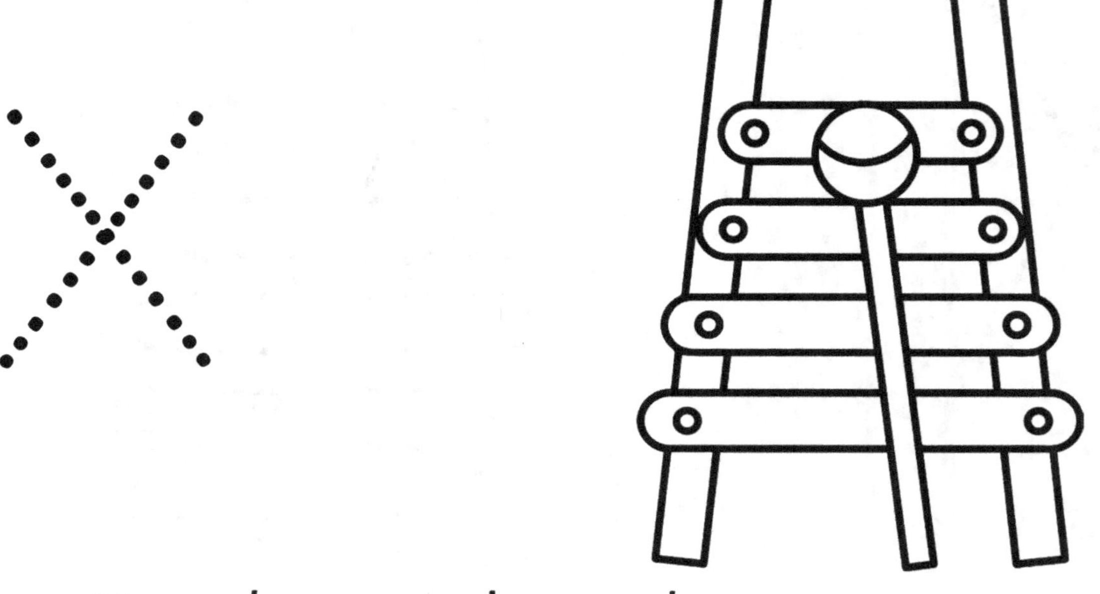

Trace the cursive letters, then write your own

Y is for Yogurt

Trace the cursive letters, then write your own

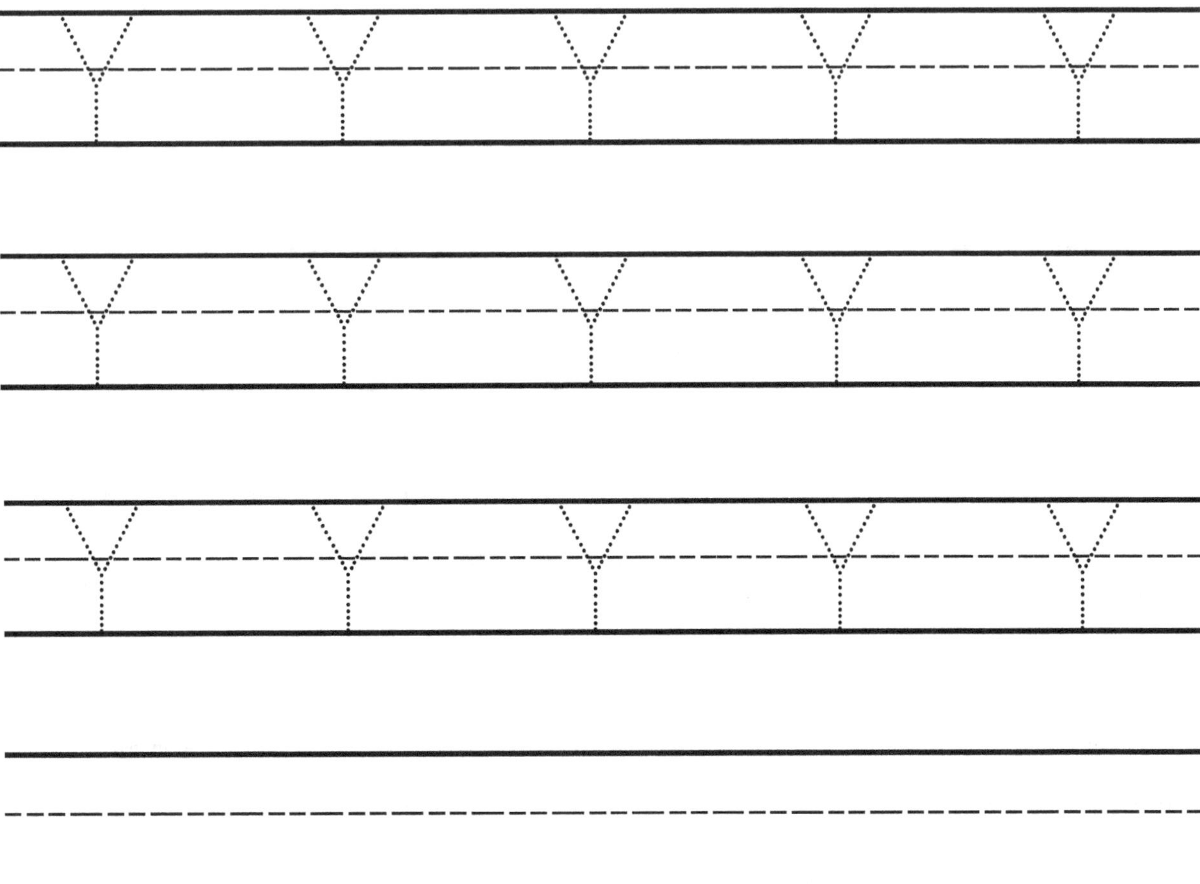

is for yogurt

Trace the cursive letters, then write your own

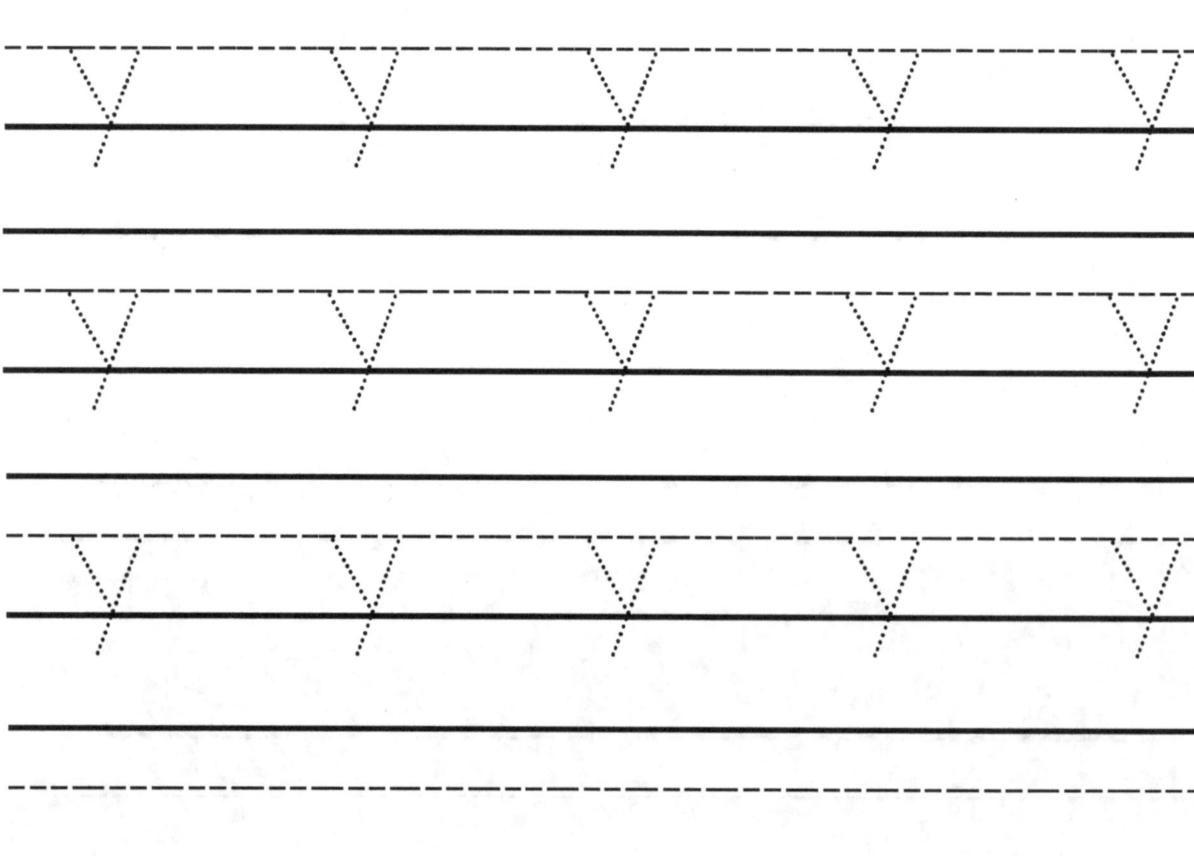

is for Zipper

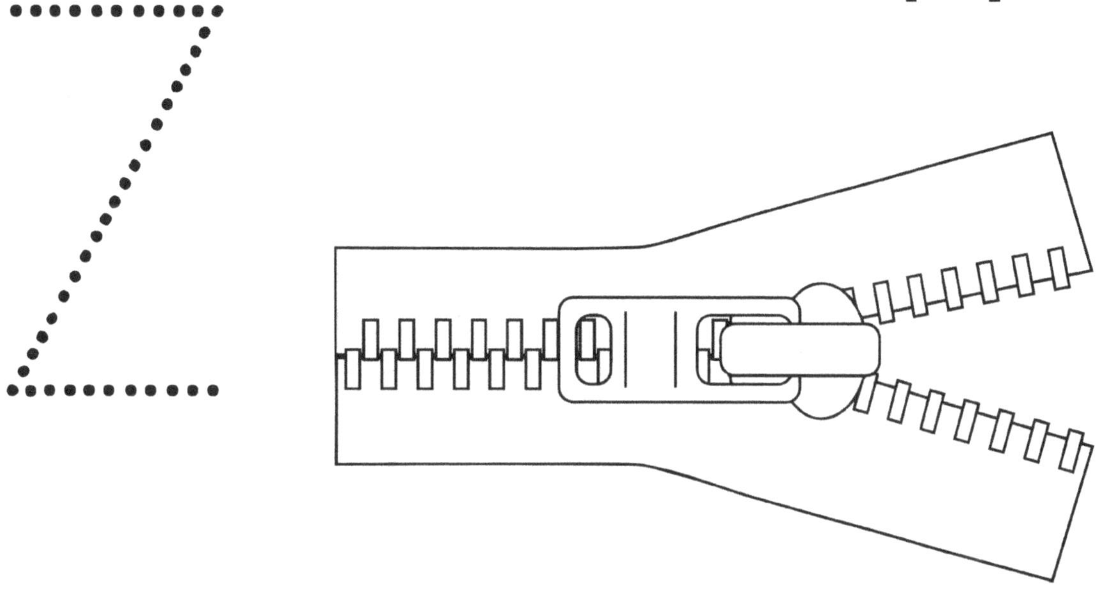

Trace the cursive letters, then write your own

is for Zipper

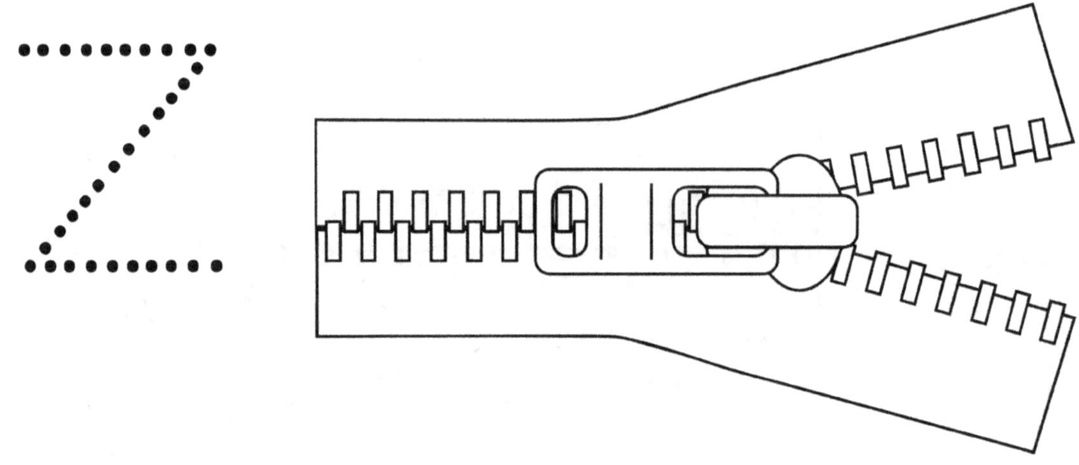

Trace the cursive letters, then write your own

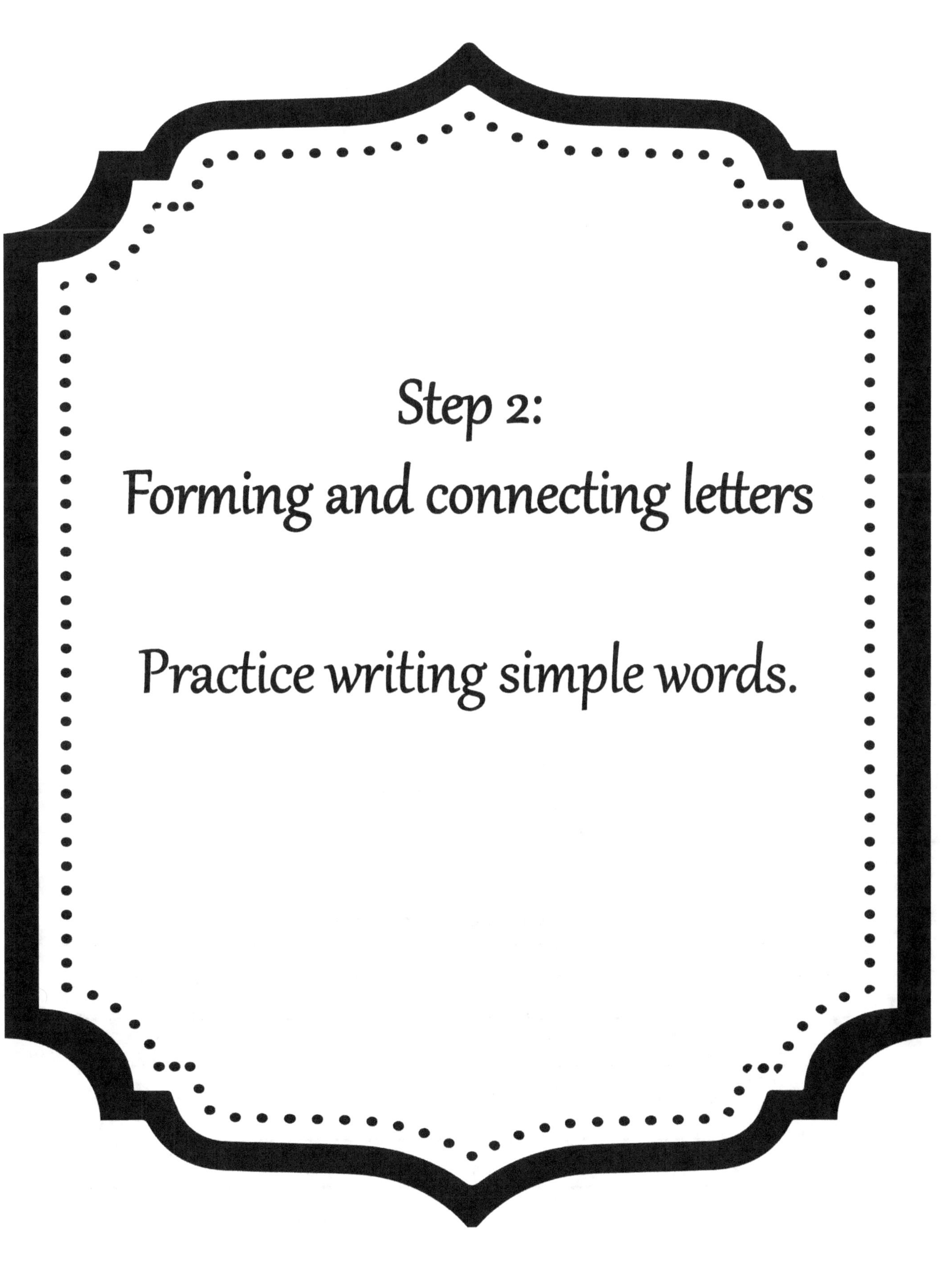
Step 2:
Forming and connecting letters

Practice writing simple words.

Star Star Star
Star Star Star
Star Star Star

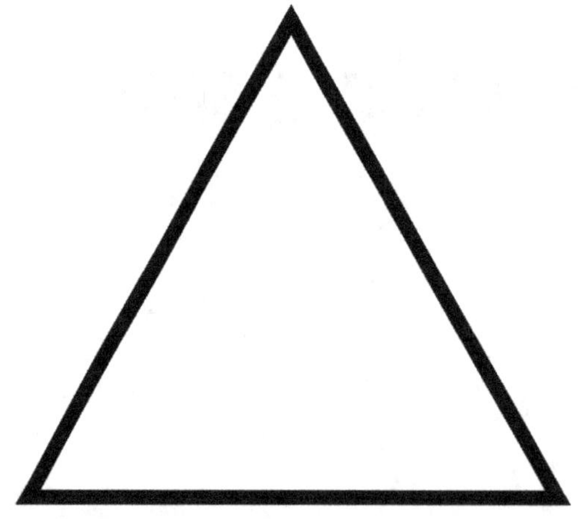

Triangle Triangle
Triangle Triangle
Triangle Triangle

Cupcake Cupcake

Cupcake Cupcake

Cupcake Cupcake

Bread Bread

Bread Bread

Bread Bread

Elephant   Elephant
Elephant   Elephant
Elephant   Elephant
Dog   Dog   Dog
Dog   Dog   Dog
Dog   Dog   Dog

Hamster Hamster
Hamster Hamster
Hamster Hamster

Chick Chick Chick
Chick Chick Chick
Chick Chick Chick

Rain Rain Rain

Rain Rain Rain

Rain Rain Rain

Sun Sun Sun Sun

Sun Sun Sun Sun

Sun Sun Sun Sun

Heart   Heart
Heart   Heart
Heart   Heart
Crown   Crown
Crown   Crown
Crown   Crown

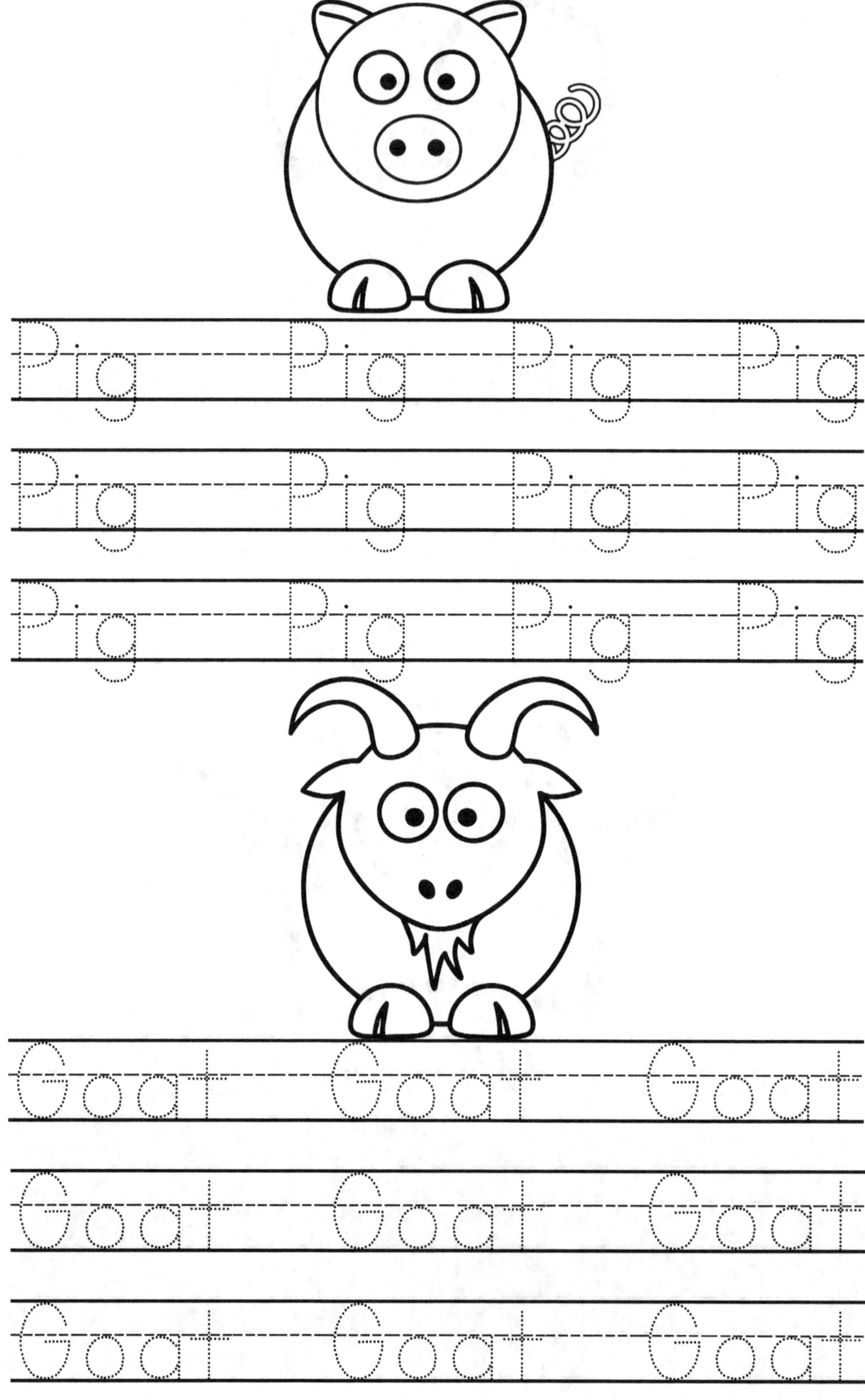

Pig Pig Pig Pig
Pig Pig Pig Pig
Pig Pig Pig Pig
Goat Goat Goat
Goat Goat Goat
Goat Goat Goat

Rainbow   Rainbow

Rainbow   Rainbow

Rainbow   Rainbow

Cloud   Cloud   Cloud

Cloud   Cloud   Cloud

Cloud   Cloud   Cloud

Candle   Candle

Candle   Candle

Candle   Candle

Cake   Cake   Cake

Cake   Cake   Cake

Cake   Cake   Cake

Dice   Dice   Dice

Dice   Dice   Dice

Dice   Dice   Dice

Balloon   Balloon

Balloon   Balloon

Balloon   Balloon

Hand   Hand   Hand

Hand   Hand   Hand

Hand   Hand   Hand

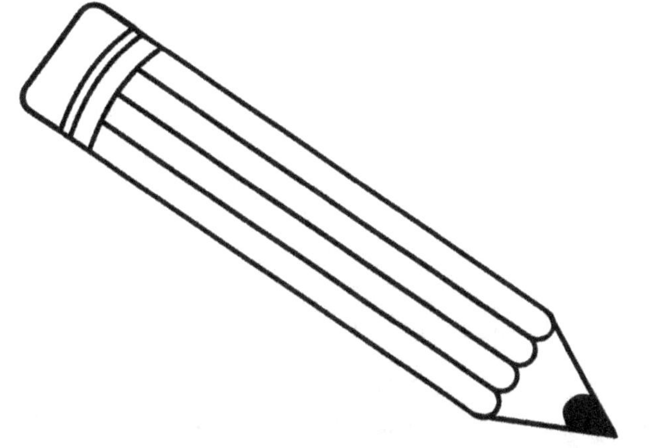

Pencil   Pencil   Pencil

Pencil   Pencil   Pencil

Pencil   Pencil   Pencil

Monkey Monkey
Monkey Monkey
Monkey Monkey
1
One One One One
One One One One
One One One One

Step 3:

Practice writing simple sentences

Enjoy!

This is a frog

This is a frog

Frogs have four legs

Frogs have four legs

Frogs can eat bugs

Frogs can eat bugs

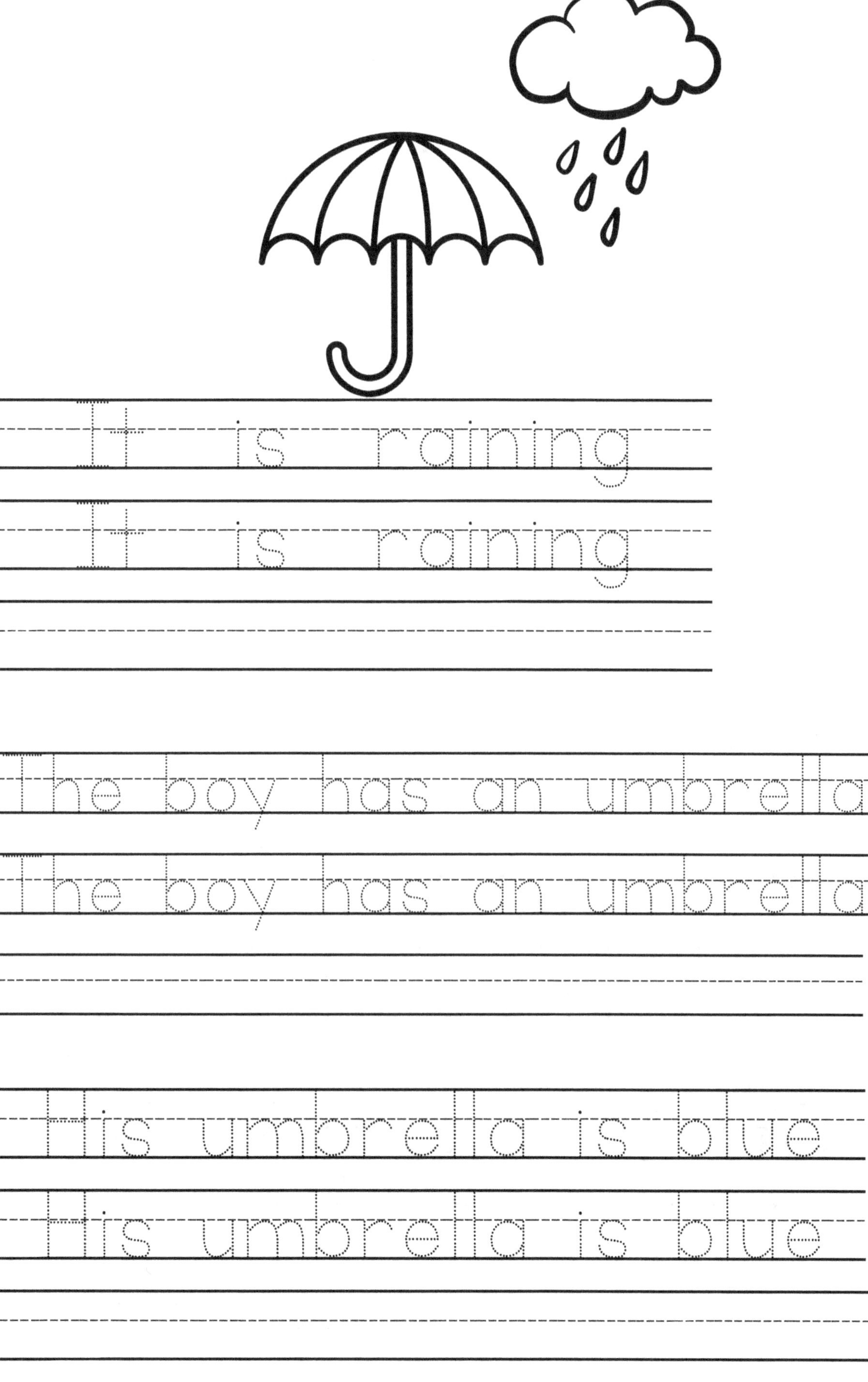

It is raining
It is raining
The boy has an umbrella
The boy has an umbrella
His umbrella is blue
His umbrella is blue

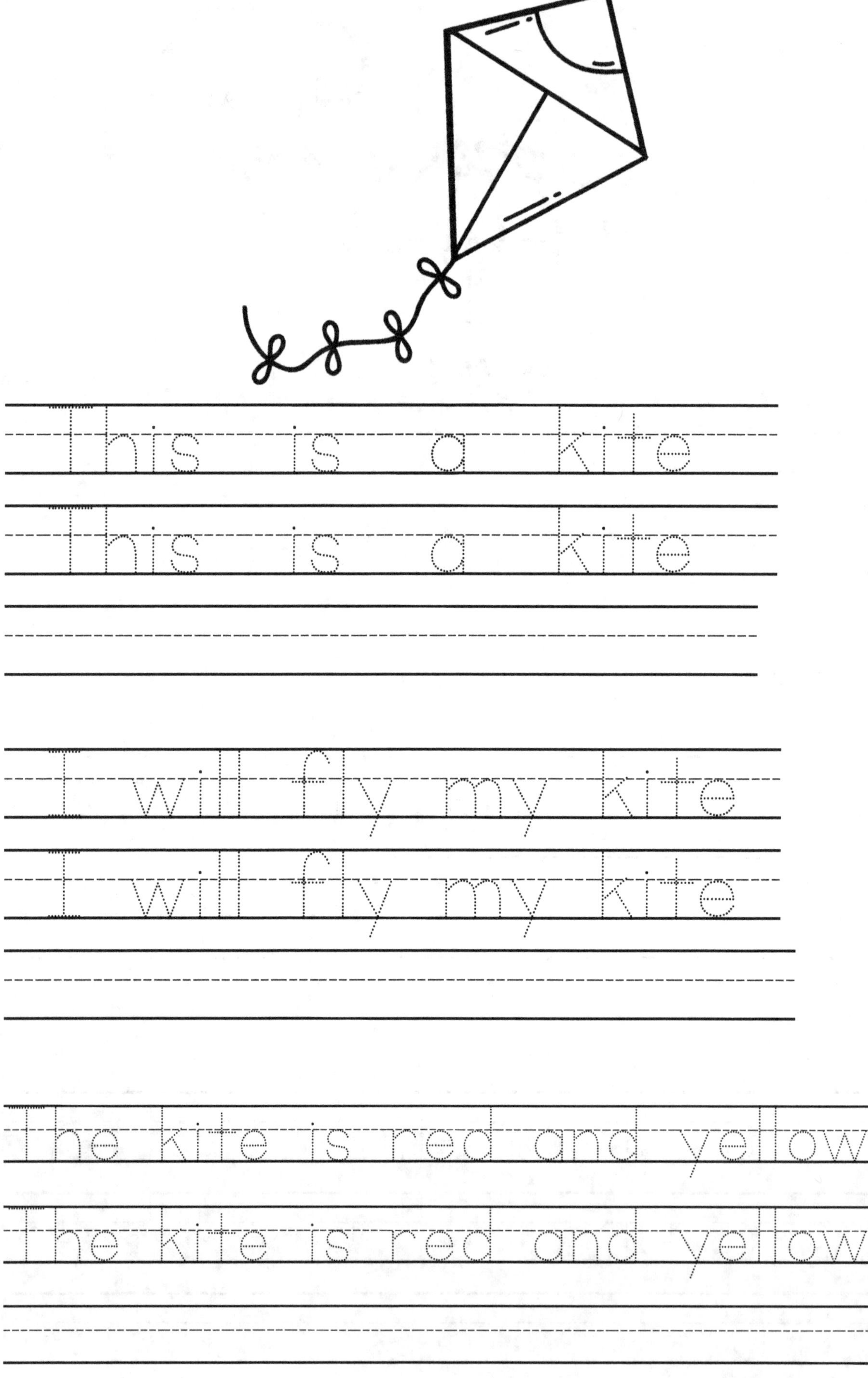

This is a kite

This is a kite

I will fly my kite

I will fly my kite

The kite is red and yellow

The kite is red and yellow

This is my friend Alice

This is my friend Alice

She wears a pink shirt

She wears a pink shirt

She has brown hair

She has brown hair

Alex has a pet

Alex has a pet

It is a beautiful cat

It is a beautiful cat

Its name is Oscar

Its name is Oscar

I see a cow

I see a cow

The cow likes to eat hay

The cow likes to eat hay

The cow is black and white

The cow is black and white

I have a fish

I have a fish

I like my fish

I like my fish

The fish is orange

The fish is orange

I see with my eyes
I see with my eyes

I hear with my ears
I hear with my ears

I taste with my tongue
I taste with my tongue

I smell with my nose
I smell with my nose

I touch with my hands
I touch with my hands

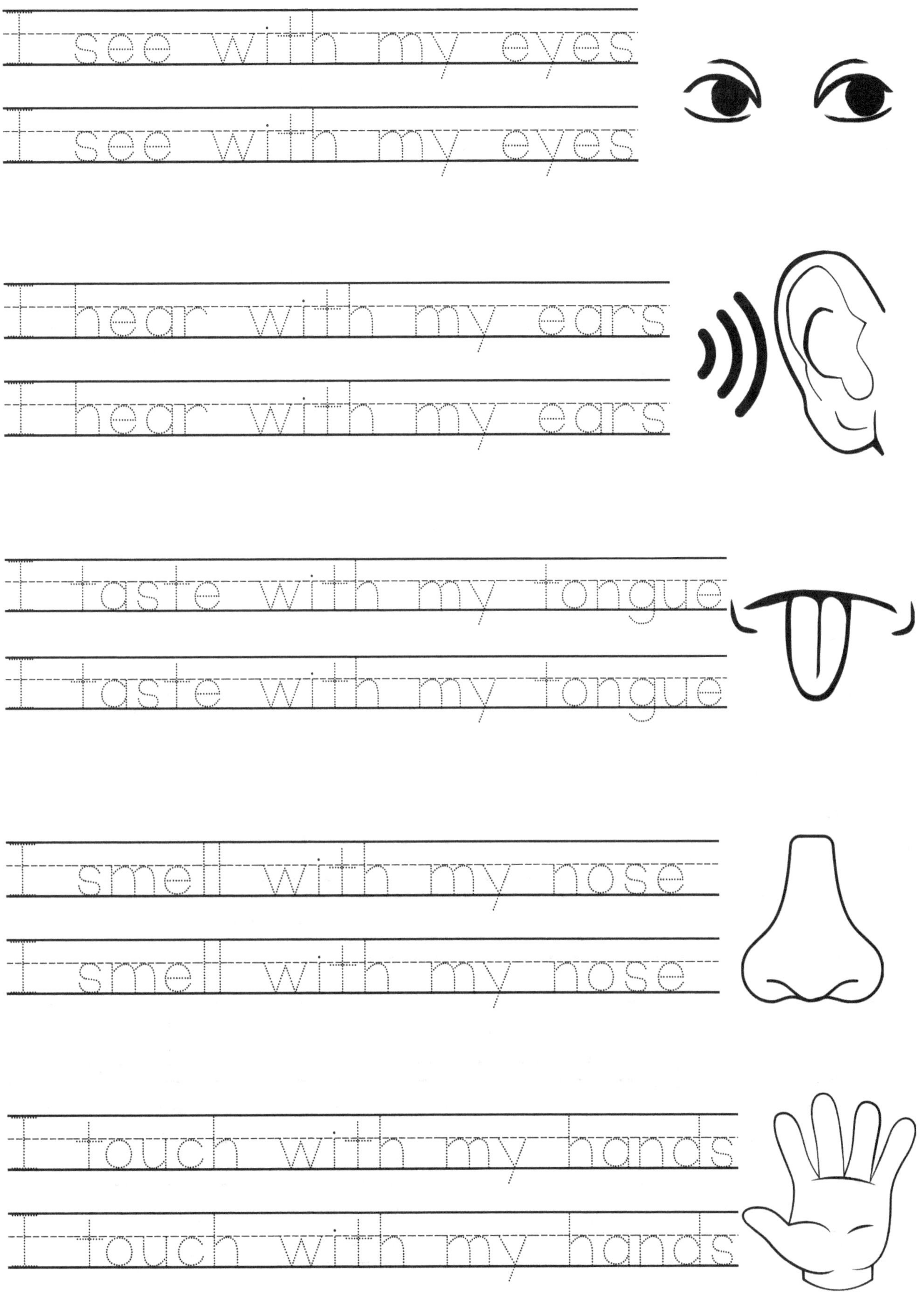

Days of the week

Sunday Sunday Sunday

Monday Monday Monday

Tuesday Tuesday Tuesday

Wednesday Wednesday

Thursday Thursday

Friday Friday Friday

Saturday Saturday

Seasons of the year

Spring Spring Spring
Spring Spring Spring

Summer Summer
Summer Summer

Fall Fall Fall Fall
Fall Fall Fall Fall

Winter Winter Winter
Winter Winter Winter

I hope you enjoyed!